The Healing of
Reverend James

Thomas John

i

The Healing of Reverend James Thomas John

DEDICATION
For my wife, Diane

PROLOGUE
Deland, Florida 1885

Reverend Carlton Amos Matthews stopped carving the large ornate oak cross that lay across the wooden bed of the horse-drawn wagon. He cocked his head to one side as he looked up above the surrounding treetops into the darkening sky. His fiery eyes scanned the blue horizon, the whites of his eyes set off by the brown pupils and the dark brown skin surrounding them. In the distance, to the east, above the small clearing in the middle of the pine trees, hung a patch of low, dark clouds. The crimson edges of the approaching storm front warned the preacher of the impending rain. A whinny rose from the front of the cart.

"Steady, Mollie," said Carlton, trying to ease the mare's unrest. Shaking off the uneasy feeling, the preacher picked up the wooden cross with reverence and carried it to the lone structure in the clearing, a small wooden chapel. Hand-hewn pine boards made up the four walls, with holes on two sides for the future windows. The roof of the chapel was also unfinished; its pine planks not yet covered with anything to shed water. Wooden stairs led up to the only door to complete the work-in-progress. Reverend Carlton Matthews climbed the handmade stairs, opened the door, and was about to enter when he stopped and backed out onto the porch, looking skyward.

As he searched the sky to the east again, he snapped his head to the north, peering through the trees. He cocked his head and listened intently. The preacher set the cross down on the porch, leaning it against the door of the tiny chapel, and continued to stare into the trees. *There it is again,* thought the preacher. *Like thunder, but not quite.* The sound definitely came from the woods to the north. The preacher crept down the stairs, his focus on the tree line, when suddenly he froze. *Horses!* The thought exploded through the preacher's brain. *A lot of horses.* That wasn't good.

Reverend Carlton jumped off the stairs and ran to his horse so fast that she began prancing in her harness. "Mollie…home!" With that, Reverend Carlton gave the mare a swat on her backside and the horse sprang into action, running south with the wagon in tow. The preacher watched until the horse and wagon disappeared from view. He turned his fifty-nine-year-old frame toward the north once again, and the large gnarled fingers of his right hand combed his graying, tightly curled hair. Reverend Carlton turned his head skyward, closed his eyes and prayed out loud, "Dear Lord, please help this sinner at the hour of his need."

The preacher heard the thundering hooves of the approaching horses; their echo growing louder throughout the little clearing as they drew near. While he peered through the twilight, Carlton reached into his pocket and withdrew an old worn leather-bound Bible. He strode back to the chapel, climbed the stairs, and turned around with his back to the wooden cross he had set there only moments earlier. The preacher pulled himself up to his full height of five feet and ten inches, placed the Bible in front of his heart, and grasped it with both hands.

The Healing of Reverend James

The pounding hoofbeats exploded; the flickering light of the riders' torches brightening the scene as they entered the clearing. Reverend Carlton stared, eyes forward, as the mounted riders circled behind the chapel, hooting and hollering as they went. Looking at the riders arriving in front of the chapel, the preacher saw that all but one of the men wore burlap sacks on their heads. The sacks had holes cut for their eyes but were poorly placed, with most of the eyeholes not lining up quite right. That gave the horsemen a garish, otherworldly appearance. One rider had white flour sacks, not only over his head, but over his horse's head as well.

The white-headed horseman stopped his steed in front of the staircase and looked down at the preacher in front of him. The other eleven riders formed a semi-circle behind him, effectively closing off any escape route for the preacher. There was silence but for the wind whipping through the trees and the crackling of the torches. The clearing was quite dark and getting darker as the approaching bank of rain clouds shut out the last streaks of light from the west. Twelve pairs of eyes glared at the black man in front of them.

Reverend Carlton Amos Matthews looked up at the group. They appeared much taller than they were; the torches sent shadows dancing across the hidden faces of the hooded men. *This is why I left Alabama,* thought the preacher, remembering the long trip south to Florida; *I should've gone north.* There was no time to think of that arduous journey now. Even though he had escaped the Klan back then, it was going to take a miracle to get out of this situation. That was just what the preacher was silently asking for when he looked to the heavens, *Lord, I need you as always. If it is your will that I die here today…so be it. Please look after my wife and son.*

Seeing the preacher's eyes turn toward the sky and watching the silent prayer made the horseman up front chuckle. Right on cue, the eleven men behind him snickered as well. "You ain't going to get any help from up there, nigger man." Their leader said. "The only thing you're gonna see above your head is the branch you're swinging from."

With that the group started hooting and hollering again, their skittish horses prancing about. The white-headed leader of the group grabbed the rope that hung from his saddle, deftly formed a loop, and in the blink of an eye, swung it up over his head. The men cheered as Whitey dropped the loop over the preacher all the way down to his ankles. A loud clap of thunder shook the little clearing as Whitey tightened the other end of the rope around the pommel of his saddle. He spurred the horse into motion, as another clap of thunder helped to jolt the horse into action as well.

The Klansmen cheered as the rope was pulled tight, slamming the preacher's body onto the stairs. Reverend Carlton was launched into the dirt and dragged away toward the trees. Half the group took off after Whitey, their torches lighting the way. While the others circled the little chapel, two men threw their torches through the window openings on either side of the structure.

The Healing of Reverend James

It took only a moment for the chapel to catch, the dried wood easy fuel for the oily flames. By the time the other group screamed and laughed back into the clearing with Reverend Carlton in tow, the sides of the wooden structure were already fully engulfed. Whitey rode his horse far enough into the clearing that Reverend Carlton's body rolled up right in front of the stairs.

The man who had lit the way when Whitey had dragged Reverend Carlton through the woods jumped off his horse. He knelt beside the bruised and groaning preacher. "He's still holding on to that Bible," shouted the kneeling man as he turned his face toward his mounted friends, "not that it's going to do him any good."

"Jimmy, watch out," shouted the rider nearest him, pointing at the ground where the preacher lay. Jimmy snapped his head around just in time to receive a massive black fist across his jaw that knocked him off his knees. He fell to the ground, stunned.

During that moment of frozen disbelief for the riders, Reverend Carlton had loosened the rope and clumsily jumped to his feet. He kicked his feet out of the loop and put the Bible into his coat pocket. Then he climbed one of the stairs toward the burning chapel where he turned around, eyes blazing, and faced his incredulous captors.

The men looked at each other, then back to the preacher. Their eyes hardened, and the growing fire in front of them added to the hideous look of their awkward, bagged faces. Skinny, the tall and slender man closest to the preacher, grabbed a long-barreled shotgun from his saddle and jumped to the ground. He cocked both hammers and drew the gun up and leveled it at Reverend Carlton.

"Stop," shouted Whitey, as he also jumped off his horse. With amazing speed, he covered the distance between the would-be shooter and himself.

"You gonna let him get away with hitting Jimmy?" responded Skinny. "That nigger is going to die *now*!" With that, the gunman looked down the barrel.

With lightning reflexes and controlled force, Whitey pulled a wooden club from underneath his clothing and cracked Skinny across the face, knocking him to the dirt. The gun discharged when he hit the ground, the lead flying harmlessly into the burning chapel. The horses jumped at the blast, and the riders grumbled as they regained control of their animals.

"He *is* going to die, you idiot, but if you shoot him, I don't get to watch him hang." Whitey glared at the shooter and then stared down the rest of the riders as well. "Now get that noose around this nigger's neck before he burns to death in that fire." The men continued to stare at Whitey for a moment too long. "Now!"

Thunder shook the trees and sparked the startled men into action. Two of the men dismounted and helped Jimmy and Skinny to their feet. They grabbed the noose and made their way toward the preacher. As the four men headed for the stairs, a great gust of wind from the southeast sent dust and pine needles flying through the air. The first two men grabbed the preacher's arms and held him while Jimmy dropped the noose over his head. Reverend Carlton did not struggle when the men dragged him off the stairs. They led him in the direction of a large maple tree at the edge of the clearing.

"Jimmy," shouted Whitey, "throw that cross into the fire."

Jimmy headed back up the stairs, bent over, and picked up the cross. Cowering from the heat of the burning building, Jimmy carried the cross around the side of the chapel. With a cheer from the men, he heaved the heavy cross up onto the flaming roof which collapsed immediately, causing the cross to fall through the burning structure. The men trembled with excitement as the side walls of the chapel collapsed. Moments later, the back wall fell outward, and the front wall crashed onto the stairs; pieces of flaming wood and embers exploded in all directions.

A forceful gust of wind blew through the clearing as thunder once again shook the surrounding area. The already spooked horses began jumping and snorting, which added to the rapidly increasing chaos. Jimmy barely saw his rearing horse in time to tumble clear of the terrified animal's descending hooves. In the process, he rolled right through a fresh pile of horse dung. The riders laughed so hard at Jimmy that a few of them nearly fell out of their saddles. The rest gasped for breath as they clung to the reins of their horses.

"Nice roll, shithead," came from the back of the group.

"You smell better now, Jimmy," came from up front, the anxious group enjoying the momentary distraction.

Jimmy picked himself up, knocked the dung off his thigh, and ignored the onslaught of comments from his so-called friends.

Reverend Carlton stood under the maple tree where his laughing Klansman captors had dragged him. He appeared unfazed by all the chaos around him, and he glared at the men, one by one. As the men became aware of the preacher staring at them, their laughter stopped. All eyes now drilled into the preacher.

The wild wind and crackling wood echoed throughout the clearing, as the men refocused on the purpose of their twilight ride. In unison, they turned their heads toward Whitey.

"Bring me the other end of that rope," directed Whitey. He extended his hand out as Jimmy grabbed the loose end of the rope. Whitey continued, "The only thing I like better than a burning cross is a hanging nigger."

The men jostled for position near the maple tree. Whitey gathered the loose end of the rope and tossed it about nine feet over his head. The rope fell over a large branch. As the group shouted encouragement to their leader, Whitey smartly wrapped the rope around his pommel and made clicking sounds to his horse. The stallion backed away from the tree, pulling the noose tighter around the preacher's neck. That lined Reverend Carlton up directly under the branch over which the rope had been thrown.

spotted a hawk. He had known that he was safe when the good Lord had pushed the rain into the Klansmen's eyes. They had not seen him as he had thrown the noose from his neck and then hidden. He had been spared, and with that fact came the knowledge that he must have more to do before his earthly time was up.

Approaching the destroyed chapel, the preacher was grateful. He was grateful that he would see his son grow, grateful that he would once again hold his wife in his arms. Most of all, he was grateful that he had been given the wisdom not to ride his horse-drawn buggy back to his house, where the men would have certainly followed him and killed them all.

He had left his previous home in Alabama almost twenty years earlier to escape these hooded killers that had sprung up right after the Civil War ended. He had thought that he would be safe this far south, but it was not to be. *I should have gone north,* thought the preacher, *so far north they wouldn't dare follow us.*

Reverend Carlton stood before his fallen chapel and surveyed the damage. His eyes came to rest on the unscathed cross. As he looked to the sky, he clasped his hands together and closed his eyes in a silent prayer of thanks. After a moment, the preacher opened his eyes and looked back down at that beautiful wooden cross, the light behind his eyes blazing anew. "Alright, then," he roared, his head rearing back, "I hear you! North it is!"

With that, the preacher bent over and carefully placed his finger on the cross. Surprisingly, it felt cool to his touch. He pulled it from the smoldering embers of his chapel and heaved it over his shoulder. Shaken but unafraid, he turned to face the wind and the rain. Bending over into the onslaught, following the path his horse and buggy had taken just a short time earlier, Reverend Carlton Amos Matthews headed home.

THE HEALING OF REVEREND JAMES

Chapter 1
Jamestown, New York 2015

Reverend James Matthews, a fifty-year-old black preacher, stood at the altar of the plain Baptist church and prayed for his own death.

Clinging to his great-grandfather's old leather bound bible in his right hand, and gripping the plain oak lectern with his left, the preacher was oblivious to the crowded pews in front of him. He did not hear the passionate verses of *Amazing Grace* being sung by the two dozen choir members behind him. He was not thinking about anything to do with life. He only saw a seven-foot-long metal box in front of him that was covered in the flowers of death. In the middle of the flowers was a photo of his only child, twenty-one-year-old John Carlton Matthews. Inside that casket, every bit as dead as his son, was Reverend James' soul.

All eyes were on the preacher, including those of Maya Richards, Reverend James' choir director of twenty-seven years. Maya thought she had seen everything. She had taken over the baton for this church at the tender age of twenty-two.

When Reverend James' wife, Thelma, had died, Maya had been forty-one. That was eight years ago, and Maya had been amazed at how the preacher had recovered. True, he was never quite the same. But with his then thirteen-year-old son, John, dreaming of

15

someday becoming a professional basketball player, Reverend James had redoubled his efforts to help his son with that goal. John was a high school standout, accepted on a full scholarship to Syracuse University, and was hopefully well on his way to the New York Knicks. Just after finishing his junior year with the Orangemen, the cancer had struck—now this. *How much can one person take?*

Reverend James' eyes saw nothing. His ears heard nothing; his mind drifted away to the memory of another day, eight years earlier....

***

He pictured himself stepping into the sun as he exited the wooden double doors of his church. His smile greeted the parishioners as they walked onto the landing and headed down the stairs into the large asphalt parking lot. The forty-two-year-old preacher shook hands and gave hugs, a Sunday ritual, until the last few churchgoers headed for their cars.

The parking lot of the Baptist church began to empty. The preacher spotted his wife, Thelma, and son, John, as they stood by Thelma's Taurus in the back corner of the lot. Nimbly bounding down the stairs, Reverend James strode across the parking lot, as his family got into their car. About halfway to the car, the preacher slowed and turned around to take in the view of the modest brick and wood building where he had spent his life. Through one of the six tall and narrow windows, he saw the altar, its familiar plain wooden charm adding to the joy of that early afternoon.

Reverend James scanned the lot for any parishioners that needed his help. Seeing none, he approached the driver's side of the Taurus to find his wife, Thelma, staring up at him through the open window. She flashed her familiar smile, her pretty face making his heart flutter even after all these years. Next to her, in the passenger seat, sat their gawky thirteen-year-old son, John Matthews. The fact that John would rather be somewhere else was evident by the size of the frown he wore for his parent's benefit. Reverend James was about to comment on John's frowning face when he heard his mother's voice, off in the distance. The preacher pulled his head from the car. A charismatic smile erupted across his strong face as he looked in the direction of the voice.

Mary Matthews, a matronly black woman of seventy-four, was chugging toward the car, shouting at her son. "Reverend James! James…wait! They can't leave until I see my grandson."

"Hello, Momma." Reverend James walked toward the back of the car, his arms spread wide in welcome. His mother bustled right past him and headed toward the passenger side of the vehicle.

Mary put on her best cherubic smile and looked down at John Matthews. "How's my favorite grandchild?"

"I'm your *only* grandchild, Grandma," growled the frustrated young man. His leg twitched impatiently as he fidgeted in his seat.

"Precisely why you're my favorite," said Mary. She reached into the car and tousled his hair. Mary Matthews looked across the seat to her daughter-in-law, "Hi, Thelma."

John pulled his head away from his grandmother's touch, and Thelma floated the usual compliment. "You're looking younger every day, Mary."

John leaned back in the passenger seat and put both of his hands over his face in obvious frustration. "Can we go?"

Thelma Matthews looked a little startled and grabbed her son's shoulder "Why, John Matthews! Mary, I'm sorry…."

Reverend James bolted around the car, his obvious displeasure at his son's lack of manners carried on the strength of his voice. "John, don't be rude to your grandmother."

His wife interrupted as she leaned across John to explain to her mother-in-law, "I'm sorry, Mary, we're late for basketball tryouts."

"Oh, don't worry 'bout me, now," laughed Mary, turning to her son. "Actually, Reverend James, he reminds me a lot of you at that age. Besides, we got a lot of time to make a preacher out of him yet." John rolled his eyes with that I've-heard-it-all-before look. "Fifth in a row," continued Mary, her smile growing at the thought, "gonna make his great-great-granddaddy proud!"

Thelma lifted her eyes skyward, "Amen."

The Healing of Reverend James

John looked to his mother, then to his grandmother. An idea crept into his brain on how to quickly get out of this situation and on his way to tryouts, "I know, I know. My great-great-granddaddy, Carlton Amos Matthews, built this stone chapel just twenty years after the Civil War, and he carved that solid oak cross—the one that's hangin' on the chapel wall—with his bare hands and the fire of his faith!" John paused for effect. *"Now* can I go to tryouts?" John wrapped his face in a cloak of innocence as he looked at his stunned relatives.

The silence was broken when Mary Matthews burst into deep, rumbling laughter, "Yes sir, Reverend James, a carbon copy of you at that age." She looked up at her son, and he put his arm around her shoulders.

Reverend James peered into the eyes of his teenage child. Unable to keep a straight face, he laughed, "Alright, alright, get out of here."

The Ford's engine came to life as Reverend James and Mary moved away from the vehicle. Thelma put the car into gear and backed out of the parking space. She pressed the brake, clicked into drive, and caught the eyes of her husband. She blew him a kiss through the closing window, then drove across the parking lot, and headed for the exit to the street.

Reverend James followed the car with his eyes as Thelma pulled away from him. Thinking about the kiss Thelma had mimed, the preacher muttered, "I love you, too."

Mary Matthews looked up at him, "What, child?"

"Nothing, Momma," replied the preacher. Then he yelled at the departing Taurus, "Make a few baskets for me, John!" The two watched for a moment as the car began to accelerate away from the church. The preacher turned and looked down into his mother's eyes. "Does he really remind you of me, Momma?"

Mary Matthews didn't get a chance to answer her son, as the sound of skidding tires came from the direction of Thelma's departing vehicle. The preacher and Mary turned and were dumbstruck by what they saw.

Thelma Matthews' car entered the intersection at the far end of the church parking lot. Mary's mouth dropped open when she saw that another car, an older Lincoln, had crashed through the stop sign and was headed directly toward the driver's side of Thelma's car. In an instant, Mary felt the blood freeze in her veins.

Reverend James was also staring in the direction of the oncoming disaster. His mind racing with the rush of adrenaline, everything seemed to move in slow motion. He sucked in a deep breath and released the kind of gut-wrenching scream that only comes from true horror, "Thelmaaaaaa!!!"

At that moment, the intersection exploded with the sickening sound of shattering glass and steel impacting steel. Thelma Matthews received the full force of the impact and was thrown violently against her son, John, both of them bouncing like rag dolls in the screaming metal deathtrap. The Taurus was picked up and thrown across the intersection; the heavier

Lincoln plowed through the car and was pushed to the opposite side of the road where it spun completely around from the force of the impact.

Both the Taurus and the Lincoln came to a stop. There was an eerie silence, except for the sound of a hubcap that rolled away from the vehicles, its hollow echo enhancing the sudden stillness.

Reverend James and Mary Matthews stood frozen, not yet able to fully comprehend what they had witnessed. Under his breath, Reverend James managed to let out a desperate plea, "Thelma?"

Reverend James took a step forward, then another. Slowly at first, then furiously, the preacher rushed toward the disabled vehicles. Mary burst into tears and followed her son. It seemed to take forever as the two ran for the intersection, Reverend James arriving first with Mary charging up well behind him.

The preacher ran past the Lincoln; his eyes focused on the driver's side door of the Taurus. He saw no movement in the car, its driver's side window blown out. There were shards of glass and pieces of metal strewn all over the intersection, the side of the Taurus crushed into the driver's seat. As Reverend James stepped towards the door, he saw blood spattered across the inside of the windshield and dashboard. He heard his mother praying and crying as she came up behind him. Mary shrieked when she saw the damage to Thelma's car. Reverend James raised his left arm and blocked her from going any further. His look held Mary in place as he took a few steps closer to the car.

Dear God, please, he silently prayed, negotiating with the Almighty, *I'll never ask for anything else if you just...*

The preacher wilted when he saw Thelma's lifeless eyes staring up at him from the interior of the vehicle, her skull broken and bleeding. His knees weak and his head reeling, the preacher felt as if he was about to fall over. He heard the creak of a car door that opened behind him. Suddenly remembering the Lincoln, Reverend James turned around and saw a slow moving foot that dropped onto the pavement. That was closely followed by an empty beer can that fell onto the asphalt and rolled noisily away, making a loud empty slap as it came to a stop against the curb.

Twenty-two-year-old Luke Jones stepped out of the Lincoln and leaned on the open door for support. The tall, wiry, scraggly white man bled heavily from the nose. He took in the scene through bloodshot eyes and tried to clear the fog out of his impaired mind. Luke looked into the preacher's eyes, "I.... I'm sorry, I..."

Reverend James coiled his body, prepared to attack the total stranger. The preacher's face revealed the compounding emotions rapidly building inside of his mind. Just before he launched himself at Luke, he heard a groan from the passenger side of his dead wife's car. The preacher whirled around and leaped toward the passenger side of the Taurus. He was unaware of the people who were beginning to arrive from all directions, coming from their cars and nearby homes. He ran up to the window, that was amazingly still intact and looked in to see his son, John, as he regained consciousness.

John awoke inside the car. He felt a warm, wet sensation on his face and brought his hands up to wipe his eyes. He hadn't yet realized the wetness he felt was his dead mother's blood. Becoming aware of a weight on his legs, John brought his hands down, and found himself staring into lifeless eyes. His brain cleared, and he recognized the crushed skull and bloody face of his mother.

Releasing an anguished scream, John Matthews recoiled backward against the passenger side glass and pushed his mother's torso off of himself. He began frantically clawing at the door while body-slamming the unrelenting glass again and again. He punched his bloody fists into the glass and tried to get away from the nightmare that was his dead mother lying beside him. "No! No! No!" John screamed. He continued to beat the glass, "Help me! Somebody, please help me!"

Outside the car, Reverend James pulled and pulled the door handle, but was unable to open the door. "I'll get you out, John. John!" The door would not respond, and the preacher put his face up against the glass hoping that his son would see or hear him. "Oh my God, please! John! John! John!..."

***

Reverend James Matthews' mind returned to the present nightmare that was his son's funeral. He stood at the lectern in front of his very concerned parishioners.

His choir director, Maya Richards, had watched him intently; it was now apparent to her that the preacher was struggling to maintain control. She saw Reverend James mouthing the words, "John...John."

Quickly, Maya pulled sheet music from the folder on the music stand in front of her and held it up for the choir to see. From the looks on their faces, they understood what was going on, and responded quickly. She tapped the stand with her baton and, with a quick glance to the organist, the music began.

Not liking the faraway sound of the preacher's words, Maya left her spot in front of the choir. She took a couple of steps toward the front of the altar to get a better look at Reverend James. She had seen this man crumble from the inside out with the loss of his wife. These past eight years, Maya had watched Reverend James vault between his son's basketball games and church activities. He had become more and more introverted, less patient, and even occasionally angry. That might have seemed normal for the average man on the street, but not Reverend James Matthews. Not this man. No matter what the problem, Reverend James had always been able to find a silver lining; "a light through the darkness," as his son, John, used to say. Now John was gone, too.

Maya's focus shifted toward the front pew where she found the target of her search. Mary Matthews had seen Maya's concern for her son. The silent conversation between the two women held Maya in place, the just-leave-him-be-look clearly understood.

It didn't help matters that Luke Jones, the drunk who had killed Thelma, had received only ten years in jail. The family had been distraught, but with no prior record and a well-rehearsed apology at the trial, that was the sentence. He had been released after serving just five years in jail. The man didn't even have the decency to move to another town, but had returned to Jamestown three years ago when he was released from nearby Elmira prison. *How was that justice?* Maya thought.

The choir continued to sing, and Maya took another long look at Reverend James. With a nod to Mary and a heavy sigh, she returned to her music stand.

Mary shifted her attention back to her son. It was not the pain she saw on her son's face that bothered her, nor was it the fact that her child was struggling with the death of his only child, her only grandchild. That was all normal. It was the haunted look in his eyes, the fear. That was a look that Mary had not seen on James' face since he had lost his childhood fear of the dark, the day James had found God. Not even the death of his wife eight years earlier had had that effect on her son. He was depressed and lonely, sure, but this...this was different. Mary bowed her head and dove inward with her concern, quickly finding that place of peace in the quiet of her mind. *After the burial, we will return to Grandfather Carlton's chapel. That will help. That has always helped.*

There was just something special about the chapel. Begun in early spring, 1887, and completed by that fall, the stone chapel looked out of place to some, enclosed as it was by the addition of the much larger house of worship. The new addition had been built around and over it, but both buildings had been there since Mary had first set foot in this church in the fall of 1959. That was the day she had met her son's father, Quentin Matthews.

She had moved to Jamestown from Erie, Pennsylvania to work as a librarian's assistant at the James Prendergast Public Library that was due to complete its expansion the following year. It was her first time to this church. She had met Quentin Matthews while he greeted the parishioners after the service. Love at first sight was an understatement. When Mary had talked to Quentin, her life had felt complete. He had felt the same way about her. The two were married just six months later, in March of 1960, and were together every day until he died of kidney cancer in April of 1994. Mary had spent every morning since on her knees, thanking God for the time they had been together and the beautiful memories.

Mary glanced up from her seat to gaze at the out-of-place-looking ten-foot-high stone chapel situated to the right and slightly behind the altar of the main church. The old wooden roof had been removed when the new addition was built in the mid-1920s. A flat roof had been installed, and that space on top of the chapel had been used for many things since then. Her favorite was the nativity scene that had been set up there every Christmas season.

Quentin's grandfather, Carlton Amos Matthews, had arrived in Jamestown, New York, in the late spring of 1886. His trek from Florida with his wife, Rosie Fielding Matthews, and their son, Abraham Lincoln Matthews, had cost the family nearly everything they'd owned. They had arrived with the clothing on their backs, an old leather bound bible, and a large wooden cross. During the trip, they had taken scraps of work, usually heavy and dirty, just for food and a place to sleep. They had sold the wagon and their beloved horse, Mollie, just to make it as far as northern Virginia.

It was family lore that in the fall of 1885, Reverend Carlton had turned down an offer of one hundred dollars for the oak cross from a wealthy white pastor in the Winchester, Virginia area. That was considered a fortune at the time. After repeatedly refusing the offer, Reverend Carlton had accepted the pastor's invitation to spend the winter months at the pastor's residence just outside of Winchester. From reading Carlton's journal, Mary knew that it was there that Reverend Carlton learned how to make walls out of stone. His then ten-year-old son, Abraham, learned the trade by his father's side.

In the spring of 1886, the preacher took his family on a winding path toward and through Pennsylvania, then up into New York State. They skirted the Indian reservation at Salamanca and arrived near Lake Chautauqua as autumn began. He and

Abraham completed the little chapel just nine months later in 1887 on the spot where the thick stone walls stood today, in the town of Jamestown, New York.

The chapel seemed almost tiny now, but at the time, the four rows of pews on either side, with the ample altar up front, served the small parish well. The cherished three-and-a-half-foot-tall oak cross hung on the updated plaster wall behind the altar. The two side walls were still finished with the original hand cut maple boards. The front wall was also original, with the exception of the newer wood and glass door that completed the structure and faced the congregation.

Mary snapped out of her thoughts about family history. Turning to her right, she saw her longtime family friend, Father Patrick Kirk. His eyes were searching her own. The priest served the local Catholic church that stood on Main Street less than a mile south from where he currently sat. White, medium built, with thinning graying hair and calm blue eyes, the fifty-year-old priest whispered the obvious question; "Is James going to make it through this?"

Together, Mary and the priest turned to look at the oblivious preacher and leaned in toward one another.

She said, "I don't know what is going to happen right now, Father Patrick, but after the wake, we're coming back to his great-grandfather's chapel."

Father Patrick nodded his approval.

Mary sat up straight, pulled her loose black jacket tighter around her shoulders, and reached up to adjust her hat. She searched the mournful faces around the room, her focus coming back to her son. Silently, she began to pray.

Chapter 2

A quarter mile from the church, an older model green, four-door Chevy Caprice chugged up the tree-lined street, headed for the church. The Chevy's engine billowed steam from under the hood as the driver pulled to the side of the road. Inside the car, a flustered Luke Jones slammed his fist into the dashboard three times and put down his driver's side window. Luke slapped the car into park and slammed his fist into the dashboard again, "How many times a week you need water? I just filled you up yesterday."

He reached for the glove compartment, talking to himself as he pulled out a bottle of Black Velvet. "I could use some wetting myself." He took a long draw of the whiskey, his usual answer to a problem. Luke reached up and loosened the plain black tie that was wrapped around the collar of his white, short-sleeved shirt. Looking down at his black pants, he noticed a small yellow stain, the remnant of this morning's fried eggs. Using the back of his hand, he tried, to no avail, to brush the stain away. Frustrated, he gave up and attempted to put the whiskey back into the glove compartment and, in the process, knocked a five-by-seven photo onto the floor. Gingerly, he reached down and picked up the photo. Luke took a long look.

The photo revealed Jennifer Santiago, Luke's girlfriend, an attractive twenty-nine-year-old Latina. Also in the picture were their two daughters; Jasmine, a ten-year-old beauty, and Morgan, a captivating, precocious child, just two years old. Tenderly, Luke held the photo and tears welled up in his eyes, "Hello, Jennifer, girls." Luke took a deep breath and tossed the photo back into the glove box, slamming his emotions and the glove compartment door back into place. "I sure hope you girls aren't sitting in the back row today."

He opened the car door and stepped out onto the side of the road. Leaving the car door open, he walked to the hood of the Chevy and shook his fist at the snorting vehicle, "You're gonna make me later than I already am."

Luke turned and looked up the street in the direction he was heading. The houses on the tree-lined street were similar in structure. One-and-a-half-story cape cods, each with minor changes made to the façade, an attempt by the builder to customize the modest homes. Through the trees, sunshine had begun to crawl down a towering church steeple, with contrasting light and shadows painting the remainder of the church. The morphing picture changed moment by moment with the rising September sun.

Luke ambled to the rear driver's side door and opened it. Reaching into the back seat, he pulled out a rumpled brown suit coat from the previous decade and draped it over his arm. He shut the back door and stepped up to the front. The front door creaked and groaned as it was forced to close, begging for some lubrication to ease the friction of lamenting metal on metal.

"Oh, shut up, you old nag!" barked Luke.

He kicked the front door and quickly regretted the spur-of-the-moment action as the pain reached his brain. He cried out with a sound like an exaggerated whimper. Quickly hobbling away from the vehicle and onto the sidewalk, he looked over his shoulder like he was expecting the car to attack again at any moment.

He put a little pressure on his foot and tested the pain level. Luke walked around in a small circle until he was satisfied that nothing was broken. Grunting with relief at his good fortune to have survived the incident with so little damage, he threw the old suit coat over his shoulder and sniffed his armpit. Judging the odor to be under control, he snuck back toward the disabled vehicle and leaned forward toward the glass. Checking the reflection he saw in the window, he licked his free hand and ran it over his head and slicked down the Medusa-looking fly away strands that made up his disheveled brown hair.

Maybe I should have taken a shower, he thought, knowing it was good that he had not. It would help with his plans for this morning. Luke looked down at his black pants and dull black shoes. Wetting a finger, he tried to remove the small yellow stain on his left leg, that he had spotted earlier. His fingers worked the fabric back and forth until he was satisfied. Standing up straight, Luke turned and squinted into the rising sun. "It's already too hot," he complained. Loosening his tie even further, he then turned and walked in the direction of the nearby church.

CHAPTER 3

Reverend James Matthews stood at the lectern. The choir had finished the selection Maya had picked out earlier, and they stood in silence and watched the motionless preacher. The silence lingered and grew more uncomfortable with each passing second. Maya Richards cleared her throat, quietly at first, then after a moment had passed, she cleared her throat a little louder.

Much to the relief of the parishioners, Reverend James broke out of his trance-like state. He looked around the room, shook his head and tried to clear the unwanted memories in his mind. His eyes seemed to focus as they landed on his mother in the front row.

Reverend James nodded to his mother, and the intensity of the look on her face helped to bring him fully into the present. His gaze shifted to the left of his mother and came to rest on Father Patrick Kirk, and he even managed a slight smile. Attempting to stand up even straighter, Reverend James surveyed the room of mostly black faces and briefly came to rest on the metal box in front of him. Reverend James lifted his eyes and looked at the congregation that stared back at him.

The six tall tinted windows on the east side of the church allowed some of the speckled streaks of light that made it through the leaves of the trees that lined Third Street to pepper the pews with shadows. He was momentarily transfixed by the surreal look the changing light gave the somber congregation as the sun continued to rise.

The preacher took a deep breath and forced himself to begin. "I'd like to thank you all for coming here today to…to honor the memory of my son, John Carlton Matthews. This early service was among the few last requests that he made. John wanted us to see the Light-through-the-Darkness, as he put it." Reverend James' agony flashed across his face. He held on tight to the lectern and closed his eyes.

The congregation held its collective breath as they watched their preacher wrestle with his pain. Each of the parishioners loved this man. He had gone to school with many of them. Reverend James had officiated at their weddings, baptized their children, and had dinner at their homes. Tears began to well in their eyes, and most of the men blinked rapidly and fought against the salty water that wanted to roll down their cheeks. The majority of the women had already lost the battle, and the tears flowed unashamed and unabated.

Families pulled each other a little closer, including a young Latina woman, Jennifer Santiago; who sat in the fourth row with her two children, Jasmine, and Morgan. The girls clung to their mother and tried to see over the three rows of people who sat in front of them.

The priest and Mary Matthews grasped hands with each other and Father Kirk placed his arm around Mary's shoulder. He needed comfort every bit as much as she.

Reverend James opened his eyes, inhaled deeply and continued, "Although he lost his battle with cancer, John put up a good fight! He is with his Creator now...." The preacher choked on his breath and struggled to hold on. Reverend James looked down at the casket, now fully bathed in the sunlight cascading through the east windows. "At least he is with his mother." The tears rolled down Reverend James' cheek. The pain was too great. He could not go on.

Maya had continued watching the preacher and already had sheet music in her hand. She held it up for the choir to see. The choir members dabbed their eyes and stood tall. Maya nodded to the organist and the opening of *Just a Closer Walk with Thee* began. Maya spun on her heel and walked the few steps forward to Reverend James. She draped her arm around the preacher and spoke into the microphone. "Baskets will be passed around. As you know from the notices we sent out, one of John's last requests was that we take a collection for the American Cancer Society that had done so much to help during his illness. Please stand and feel free to join us in song as you give."

The congregation rose.

Maya glanced to the far right of the front row and found the women she had asked to pass collection baskets.

The Burton twins, Shawna and Shannon, left their seats, their matching black outfits accentuating their slender, curvy figures. Thirty-four-year-old women of color, they held the baskets they had received from Maya when they had arrived at the church. Each adjusted her black hat and walked to the aisle that divided the pews in two at the center of the building.

The people on the insides of the rows, nearest the twins; Shannon on the east side of the aisle, Shawna to the west, took the baskets that were handed to them. They retrieved their donations and dropped the cash into the baskets, then passed the baskets to the people next to them. The love felt for John Matthews was reflected by the large denominations being dropped into the baskets as they were handed from person to person. The baskets arrived at the ends of the rows, and the last person in each row dropped in a donation, then turned and handed the basket to the person in the row behind. Shannon and Shawna took a step toward the back of the church, keeping pace with the baskets as they advanced from row to row. Shawna noted Maya's wisdom in giving them the largest baskets available.

Not one person turned around when the back door of the church opened and revealed a hunched-over Luke Jones. Head down, he crept in. The church door closed by itself while Luke slid behind the back pew. He coughed and hacked his way across the back aisle, putting on the rumpled suit coat as he went. Luke continued to increase the volume of his coughing as he came around the corner of the west aisle, stood outside the second-to-the-last pew and coughed through an uncovered mouth. To escape the torrent of disease they pictured flying in their direction, the people in that row covered their mouths and moved over. Luke stepped into the vacated space.

Luke kept up the coughing jag. Leaning out from his location against the west wall, he saw a large hulk of a black man, ten rows in front of him, dropping two twenty-dollar bills into the collection baskets. *Perfect timing!* Luke stopped coughing, and his eyes popped open with delight. He reminded himself that for his plan to work, he needed to keep up the act. Having seen the money, Luke had momentarily forgotten how sick he was supposed to be. He started hacking again as the basket continued to travel back and forth across the pews.

The people around Luke moved as far away from him as the crowded space would allow. They huddled ever closer together, certain the man next to them was about to deposit a lung on the church floor. They had trouble hearing the twenty-four-person choir that was singing from the altar.

Luke reached into his pants pocket and withdrew a one-dollar bill. He held the bill up high in his right hand. Anyone who might have looked in his direction would see that he had done his part. He could not believe how well the plan had worked to this point. His throat was dry and scratchy, but he could take care of that later. Right now, he needed to stay focused.

A subtle glance down the outside aisle revealed the basket was five rows in front of him and moving quickly. He leaned back into his row and the bottom fell out of his stomach as he looked toward the center aisle. His eyes met the eyes of Shawna Burton through a gap in the five rows of people between them. *Shit,* thought Luke, *she's staring at me!* He quickly turned away, raised his right hand higher and used the dollar bill in a lame attempt to hide his face. He bent over and coughed even louder and considered canceling his plan. *To hell with that,* thought Luke, *I gotta get some cash.*

He had borrowed money from the local loan shark, Jesus; "Hey-sous" was how the Latino community pronounced the name, and Luke was long overdue. Jesus Juarez was not known for his patience. The thought of broken bones was motivation enough for Luke. Totally lost on him was the irony of the spelling of the loan shark's name.

***

When Shawna had seen Luke Jones walk through the back door of the church, she had talked herself out of believing it. She had glanced at her sister, Shannon, and seen that Shannon was focused on her collection basket. *Luke Jones! It can't be,* Shawna had thought.

She had looked toward the sound of severe coughing in the back of the church, along the west aisle, and there he was again. *The nerve of that man to show up here,* thought Shawna, *and on the day of John Matthews' funeral!*

Shawna watched the basket as it came down the row. It was nearly full, but she believed there was enough room left in the basket for donations to make it through the last four rows. She looked toward where she had spotted Luke just a moment earlier, but too many faces blocked her view. She knew Luke had received a ten-year sentence for killing Reverend James' wife, Thelma. *Ten years for killing one of the sweetest women that ever walked the earth*! Luke had served just five years and been released for being a "model prisoner." *Dear Lord, forgive me, but that just doesn't seem fair.*

With his left hand, Luke pulled a dingy white handkerchief from his left rear pants pocket and sneezed into it. His heart thumped in his chest when he watched the basket being handed to the man in front of him, one row up. The basket traveled away from Luke and continued its hand-to-hand journey. His row was next. Out of the corner of his eye, Luke saw that Shawna Burton had stepped into view at the end of his row and glared directly at him.

The basket rounded the corner into the second-to-the-last row. *Here we go,* thought Luke. He held the dollar bill in his right hand between his two little fingers. The woman next to Luke received the basket as he sneezed hard into the hanky. The woman looked away from Luke while she covered her mouth and handed him the basket. Luke grabbed the basket with his right hand and sneezed again, pulling the basket into his belly and shielding it from view with his unbuttoned suit coat. He dropped the hanky out of his left hand, into the basket, and snatched it right back up again, a little heavier than when he dropped it. Luke curled the hanky in his left hand under the open suit coat and turned to the man behind him and handed him the basket. The man grabbed the basket and watched as Luke ceremoniously dropped the one-dollar bill into it. The man stared for a second and Luke coughed directly into his face and then turned around.

The man grunted his disgust while Luke busied himself shoving the handkerchief into his left front pocket, being careful to use the suit coat to block Shawna's view. Luke began another coughing jag as he looked down the row and found Shawna still glaring at him. He smiled at her and continued to hack and wheeze.

Shawna had suspicions that something just wasn't right. She had thought about asking the man behind Luke if he had seen Luke take anything out of the collection basket. But she was interrupted by the woman at the end of the row handing her the nearly full basket. Shawna took the basket and decided not to make a scene. After all, she had just watched Luke drop paper money into the basket. *Let it go,* she thought. *Probably nothing.*

Shawna turned to find Shannon waiting for her. The two sisters walked down the center aisle and up to the left side of the altar, and placed the money on a maple drop-leaf table that Maya had designated prior to the service. The twins gawked at the cash, turned and gave each other a wow-that's-a-whole-lot-of-money look, and returned to their seats.

Having seen Shawna turn and walk away, Luke stumbled out into the aisle and coughed and hacked his way behind the last row. He kept his head low and opened the back door of the church. He slipped out the exit and rapidly became a dim memory; the back rows of parishioners content to have had the flu-infested man disappear.

The Healing of Reverend James

As the choir finished the spiritual, Reverend James turned to Maya and grabbed her hand and hung on tight. The congregation stood and watched the moment, not sure what to do next.

Two-year-old Morgan Jones tugged on her mother's dress and whispered, "Mommy, can I sit down, now?" Jennifer Santiago looked down at the restless child and quietly chastised her daughter, "Morgan, hush up. *Un momentito, mi amorcita.*"

Reverend James released his choir director's hand, whispering, "Thank you, Maya."

She gave him a hint of a smile, backed away, and walked over to the collection baskets.

The preacher put his arms up and motioned everyone to sit. "Please. Everyone sit down." He glanced over at Maya and watched her pick up the baskets and walk through the door behind the choir, that led to the church offices.

The crowd found their seats.

"Thank you all for your generosity while honoring John's last wish. On behalf of the American Cancer Society, I thank you again. We will continue the service graveside at Hilltop Cemetery. Would the pallbearers please come forward at this time?"

The six men, including Father Patrick Kirk, rose and took their places on either side of the casket. Two more men walked to the back double doors of the church and opened them. The sun brightened the entire room as the men held the doors and prepared for the procession out to the waiting hearse. The side doors were opened as well to allow the parishioners an easy exit to the parking lot on both sides of the church.

The organist began playing the exit music, and the six pallbearers rolled the coffin in line with the center aisle. They lifted the coffin off its base and walked slowly down the aisle. The moment had come. John Matthews, the only child of Thelma and Reverend James Matthews, was carried through the open doors, leaving his beloved church for the final time.

CHAPTER 4

Luke Jones exited the church and walked across the parking lot toward his disabled Chevy. He stopped at the corner of the lot and retrieved the hanky from his left pocket. Glancing over his shoulder and seeing no one, he hunched over anyway and allowed the suit coat to act as a shield, just in case. Using both hands, he uncovered his bounty. Luke whistled when he saw the first denomination. "A hundred-dollar bill!" he shouted out loud and then scowled at his outburst. He surveyed the surrounding area again. Content no one was watching, he unraveled the handkerchief completely and revealed seven more crumpled greenbacks; two twenties, one ten, three fives, and a one-dollar bill. "Hell yeah, it's gonna be a great day!"

Luke took the hundred-dollar bill and folded it in half. Bending over and pulling up his pant leg, he stuffed it into his left sock. He pulled the rest of the money out of the handkerchief and tossed the rag onto the asphalt. In the palm of his hand, he straightened the cash, in order of denomination; two twenties first, then one ten, three fives, and last, the lowly one. *I even got my dollar back.* Luke smiled at the thought. He folded the wad and placed it in his right front pocket.

Luke heard the church doors open behind him and saw two black men dressed in suits step out onto the landing and hold the doors open. He jumped off the pavement and bolted for the sidewalk. "Time to go," he said to out loud. He took his jacket off and threw it over his right shoulder.

***

Luke was in a fantastic mood. While he walked, he played the old schoolyard game, step on a crack, break your mother's back. He had a spring in his step and even laughed when he lost his balance and almost stepped on a crack. The sidewalk was in sorry shape, and it was a challenge to avoid them all. One block away from his car, the fun stopped. He looked up to see flashing lights from a Jamestown police cruiser that was parked behind his Chevy. He was well known to the local police force, and he knew there was no point in running or hiding. He'd broken his mother's back at least a dozen times before he got close enough to realize he was in luck.

The female officer who stepped out of the patrol car was his first cousin, Shelly Jones. *Damn,* Luke thought, *I gotta play the Powerball tonight. This is the luckiest day of my life.* Ten full-time officers worked for the Jamestown police force, and nine of them would love to cause Luke trouble, but not Shelly. The two cousins had grown up together and were inseparable through their early teens. They hardly talked anymore, but Shelly still had a soft spot for Luke. She was the only member of his family who did.

Luke pasted a big smile on his face and approached Shelly with open arms to offer a hug. Shelly stopped and put her hands on her hips. That gave Luke his first clue that things might not work out as well as he hoped. Dressed in her gray and black uniform and comfortable black shoes, Shelly stood five feet, five inches tall and weighed just four pounds over a hundred. Her pale complexion and thin round face set off intense blue eyes that were currently covered by special-order Ray-Ban glasses with transitions lenses. Her chestnut brown hair was pulled back in a bun and tucked neatly under her standard-issue cap. The serious look on her face and the gun on her hip left no doubt that she meant business.

"Luke, what in the hell have you been up to?"

Luke's arms fell along with his cheesy grin. *She knows,* was the thought that popped into his brain. *Can she see the church from here?* Luke turned to look back up the sidewalk toward the church but jerked back around when he heard the intensity of his cousin's voice.

"You look at *me* when I'm talking to you, Luke Jones. You're in serious trouble." Shelly reached around behind her back and pulled handcuffs from the leather pouch that hung from her belt. "Put your hands behind your back."

Luke stood frozen in place. His head raced and his mouth moved, but no sound came out. The memories of five years in prison flashed through his mind. Getting arrested for a parole violation would send him back for—.

Luke was jolted out of his mental trauma by the sound of Shelly's laughter. He watched her as she put the hand cuffs back in place. She had laughed so hard that she momentarily lost her balance and stumbled.

"You should have seen the look on your face, Cousin Luke," Shelly gasped and tried to breathe, "I seriously thought you were going to pass out." She slapped herself on the knees and thoroughly enjoyed herself at her cousin's expense. She continued to chuckle, "Gotcha." Then she laughed some more.

"That wasn't funny," Luke deadpanned, "I thought you were serious."

"Guilty conscience, huh? Why, who'd you rob?" Shelly asked.

Luke had had enough of the conversation that had gotten far too close to the truth. "Come on, Shell, knock it off, will ya? I got places to be."

Shelly looked at the broken-down Caprice that sat at the curb and decided she'd had her fun for the day. "You out of water again?"

"Yeah," he replied, shaking his fist at the car. "Second time in two days. I tell you, you old nag, I'm gonna get me a foreign girl, you keep this crap up."

The two cousins laughed at Luke's empty threat. Shelly looked up at him and gently put her hand on his shoulder. "I've got some water in the trunk, Luke. Let's get you back on the road before my supervisor drives by." She headed for the trunk of her car. She stopped along the way, reaching through the open window of her patrol car to switch off the flashing lights.

***

Around the corner and almost out of sight from Luke and Officer Shelly was a black BMW 740Li sedan, the three men inside glued to the interactions

46

between the two cousins. The driver of the vehicle was Tony Sanghetti. Twenty-nine-year-old Tony and Luke Jones had been best friends in high school. At six-foot-two and two hundred one pounds, the rugged good looks of the high school football standout had been ravaged when Tony had driven his car into a tree. That had happened the night before he was to leave for Penn State. One hundred twenty-three facial stitches, two crushed vertebrae, and a shattered ankle had ended Tony's receiving career that evening. It wasn't his fault. The tires just couldn't hold the corner at ninety-five miles an hour.

In the passenger seat next to Tony sat Raymond Guerrero. At Six-foot-five and two hundred sixty-five pounds, Raymond was pure rippled muscle with only four percent body fat. Raymond looked like the only thing he enjoyed more than working out was consuming steroids. He had broad shoulders, a thick, tree trunk neck, and a very short fuse. He was street smart yet intellectually challenged. He was thirty-six but told the ladies he was twenty-nine. No one ever corrected him.

Tony and Raymond wore matching black Dockers, with black socks and black leather shoes. Tony liked the long-sleeved button-down shirts and sported a blue and ivory vertical striped Tommy Hilfiger. Raymond liked short-sleeved polos, the tighter the better, and always black.

In the driver's-side back seat was Jesus Julio Juarez. The forty-two-year-old bookie and loan shark wore only expensive suits that cost more than the cars most of the people in this neighborhood could afford. He had a dozen fine handkerchiefs in every color of the rainbow embroidered with his initials. He loved the way the JJJ looked sticking out of the breast pocket of the flawlessly tailored suits he purchased. The burgundy suit and pink handkerchief he wore today would look out of place here. He didn't worry about that. The only time he left the car was to go to fine restaurants, an arts venue, or home. Getting out of the car was what he paid the two goons up front to do. They were looking at their next assignment.

The men watched Officer Shelly Jones, who closed the hood of the Chevy and signaled for Luke to crank it over. The car whined and belched but started right up in spite of the complaining. Shelly stepped up on the sidewalk and waved to Luke as he pulled away from the curb. She watched the Chevy turn right and head off down the street, and then walked to her trunk and put the water container inside. The officer shut the trunk and got into her patrol car, then drove through the intersection in front of the three men.

Tony looked into the rear view mirror and into the eyes of his boss. "You want me to follow Luke?"

"No, Tony. Not now." Jesus looked down the street in the direction Luke had taken. "He'll be at the bar the rest of the day. Besides, I have a lady friend waiting for me at the house. She's young and impatient." Jesus liked to keep his women waiting for him, and he smiled at the thought of how feisty she would be when he finally arrived. "Take me home and finish your rounds. Then tonight you can have a little talk with your old friend Luke."

Tony shook his head. "We're not friends, anymore…ancient history."

"Glad to hear that. I wouldn't want friendship to get in the way of business." Jesus looked over to the passenger seat. "Take Raymond with you."

Raymond didn't move. "You want anything broken?"

Jesus was quiet, and the men waited. They never asked Jesus a question twice. If he wanted it repeated, he'd ask. They never asked about his women, either. Tony's mind wandered to the lady friend that waited for Jesus at the house and wondered if the lady was even a woman. The women Tony had seen with Jesus had looked very young, maybe too young. His thoughts were interrupted when Jesus answered. "Nothing broken this time, Raymond, but you let him know, in no uncertain terms, that he has two weeks, that's it."

Raymond grunted his understanding.

"If he doesn't have the money by two weeks from today, time's up." Jesus leaned forward to talk into Tony's right ear. "And Tony, if he doesn't pay up—*you* are going to break his kneecaps, understood?"

Tony felt Jesus' breath on the back of his head. He put the BMW into gear and answered, "Understood." Tony drove down the street and headed for the house, the sound of Raymond's and Jesus' laughter echoing in his ears.

CHAPTER 5

Returning from the burial and subsequent collation for John Matthews, three cars pulled into the west entrance of the empty parking lot of the Baptist church and made their way to parking spots near the side entrance. The early evening sun had fallen toward the horizon and stretched the shadows of the trees well into the asphalt. Mary Matthews parked her silver Ford Focus in the spot nearest the church. Father Patrick Kirk parked his black Toyota 4Runner in the spot directly behind Mary, and Reverend James pulled his green Jeep Liberty in beside his mother.

Mary Matthews worked herself out of the Focus and charged across the pavement and onto the sidewalk. She strode up to the side door of the church and, without looking back, opened the door and entered the building.

Reverend James and Father Kirk exited their vehicles simultaneously and closed their car doors. Both men stood and looked at the church door that Mary had disappeared through, then back to each other. Father Kirk walked over to his friend and put his arm around his shoulder. "She's really worried about you."

Reverend James shrugged his friend's arm off his shoulder. He walked around the front of his Jeep and headed for the church.

Father Kirk followed the preacher. "James, please, don't walk away from me like that." Reverend James showed no sign of slowing down, and the priest jogged up behind him, reached out, and spun him around, "You are NOT the only person that is hurting here!" The preacher hesitated, and Father Kirk continued, "Please give me a chance to talk, James. I didn't get a chance to talk to you at the collation, and frankly, it felt like you were avoiding me."

Reverend James planted his feet. "I wasn't avoiding you, Patrick."

The priest said nothing and continued to bore into the preacher's eyes.

Reverend James held his gaze for a moment more, then looked at the ground and shuffled his feet. "Okay, Patrick, maybe I was avoiding you," he said.

There was a moment of silence while Father Kirk continued to stare into the eyelids of his longtime friend.

Reverend James sucked in a breath and dropped his shoulders in surrender, "Okay, Patrick, you win. I *was* avoiding you."

"There is no winner in this, James. We all lost today." Father Kirk placed his hands on the preacher's shoulders and softened his tone, "I know I can't fix this. No human can. I just want you to know that I will be here for you, any time, day or night. You call; I'll come, alright?"

Reverend James nodded his head. "Alright, Patrick…alright."

Father Kirk lifted his arms off James' shoulders and spread them wide, offering a hug. The preacher accepted the invitation and fell into the priest's arms, holding on tightly. The men embraced each other in silence, gaining strength from each other.

Father Kirk stepped back. "You know I loved John. The whole congregation loved him."

Reverend James nodded again.

"There is nothing I can say that will bring him back, James. All I can do is pray that you understand you are not alone."

"I know, Patrick. I know." The preacher winced and looked to the sky, "I wish I could understand why. Why did it have to be John? So young—so talented, he had so much to give to the world." The preacher continued his search of the heavens and appeared to be waiting for a response. It came from Father Kirk.

"You and I have been asked that same question hundreds of times, James, maybe thousands. Do you remember what you told the people that asked?"

The preacher brought his face out of the clouds and glared at the priest. He opened his mouth to speak and then shut it as he changed his mind. He shifted his weight from leg to leg and looked down at his feet again.

Father Kirk was worried about his friend. They had become close almost immediately on the day they'd met. Reverend James and a very pregnant Thelma Matthews had arrived at the small Catholic church on Patrick's first day at the rectory in March of 1994. They'd come with a fruit basket and a single white rose. Patrick had assumed the white rose had significance related to Easter since they had met one week before Good Friday. Later, he learned that it was Thelma's favorite flower. Ever since the couple had been married in September of 1990, they had welcomed new clergy from every denomination to the Jamestown area in the same manner.

During their brief conversation that day the men had found out that not only were they the same age, but they also shared the same birthday, October 11, 1964, a Sunday. *Was that prophetic?* The priest would have to consider that later. Right now, there was another matter to attend to, and he was standing right in front of him.

Father Kirk had counseled thousands of people during his tenure. He could tell when a person wasn't ready to talk, and he was looking at one now. "Look, James," he began, "Mary is waiting for you in the chapel. I can tell that this moment may not be the best time to have this conversation."

Reverend James kept his eyes to the pavement and nodded.

Silence.

"So I'll be heading back to my church. I've got a number of things to finish before my day is done." The priest hesitated as a random car glided by on the quiet street. Father Kirk tracked the car during the awkward silence. It turned at the end of the block and disappeared around the corner. He looked at the sullen preacher and decided it was time to go. "Just remember what I said, James. Call me when you're ready to talk."

Father Kirk turned and walked back to his car. He was about to get in when the preacher's voice made him pause.

"Patrick." Reverend James managed to look the priest in the eyes. "Thank you."

Father Kirk, the concern etched into his face, gave his friend a slight smile and nodded. He plopped down in the front seat and drove out of the parking lot.

Reverend James watched Father Kirk drive away. He turned toward the church door his mother had entered. With a heavy sigh, the preacher walked toward the door and went inside.

CHAPTER 6

"James, I knew you would get through it." Mary Matthews had strategically placed herself in front of the chapel altar with Grandfather Carlton's cross visible over her shoulder when her son had entered the chapel. It was the perfect backdrop for their conversation.

"I'm glad you thought that, Mother. For a while there, I wasn't sure I was going to make it."

Mary pounced. "I didn't say I was proud of the way you did it."

Reverend James felt as if he had been punched in the gut. The disappointment in his mother's face and the stern tone of her voice combined to make the invisible blow.

"Your great-grandfather Carlton Amos Matthews built this chapel just twenty years after the Civil War ended," Mary continued. "Before he was dead he buried first his stillborn daughter, and then his wife.... When others would have given up, he carried on."

The preacher looked at the tops of his shoes. His action matched the behavior of a three-year-old child, and his emotional mind-set wasn't far from that.

Mary stepped in close to her son, "Your father, God rest his soul, used to say that his granddaddy Carlton carved that cross with his bare hands and the fire of his faith." Mary reached her right hand out and cupped it under his chin. She gently, but firmly, pulled his face up so she could look into his eyes. "I don't see no fire in your faith, James."

Reverend James pulled his chin out of his mother's hand and fought to keep his voice calm. "I've heard that story a thousand times, Momma…"

"—a thousand times, Momma." Mary finished the sentence with him. "And you've forgotten it a thousand and one. Now, look at that cross, child."

"Momma, please."

"You look at that cross, James!"

Reverend James forced himself not to roll his eyes and did as he was instructed.

"You've got four generations of preacher's blood in you—Matthews' blood. You've never gotten over losing Thelma. That was eight years ago. Eight years!" Mary hesitated. The reaction from her son was hard to watch. Instinctively, she knew she must continue. *Tough love.* "I've watched your pain. I watched it, and I don't like where it's taking you. Remember, James, you didn't bury just your only child, today…you buried my only grandchild."

Sucking in a breath, Mary held back the tears and prayed for the strength to go on.

Reverend James' eyes were drawn to his mother.

"I watched the cancer take your father, and it took John from us, too. I didn't let it take my faith, and I won't stand by and watch it take yours!"

The preacher grabbed his mother's hand. It was the first moment that day he had cared about any human's emotion other than his own.

Mary blazed forward, and the strength of her voice echoed throughout the chapel, "You are the

56

fourth generation in an unbroken line of Matthews preachers! Find your faith, child! Find it now. You are angry at the will of God, and that is no place for a Matthews preacher to be!"

Mary clutched her chest and wobbled a bit.

Reverend James reached out and steadied her. "Momma, are you okay?"

Mary walked a step and grabbed the back of the pew closest to her. "I'll be fine, James." She took a deep breath. "Just a little dizzy spell...I should know better—getting all worked up like that."

"Do you want to sit down, Momma?" He indicated the closest pew. "Here, sit right here."

Mary shook her son's arm off her. "I'm fine, James, really." She walked around her son to the door of the chapel and talked over her shoulder when she opened it, "I need to go, and you need some time alone to pray." Mary didn't wait for a response. She walked into the church and toward the exit. The door closed with a dull thud.

Reverend James looked through the glass window of the chapel door and considered following his mother. Personal experience decided against it. He turned and searched his great-grandfathers' cross. *Just a block of wood—beautifully carved, yes, but still just a block of wood.*

He walked over to the second row and sat in the middle of the pew. Reverend James, alone and exhausted, folded his hands on his lap and began to pray.

***

Mary Matthews climbed into her car, trying to catch her breath. She grabbed the steering wheel and held on waiting for the dizziness to subside. That wasn't the first time she'd had a "spell," as she called them. *I'm finally slowing down,* she thought. *Eighty-two years old and still kicking.* Mary knew how fortunate she was to have survived this long with near perfect health. A little dizziness wasn't going to stop her from helping her child.

Mary closed her eyes and asked her God to help her son in his hour of need. She put her car in gear and pulled out of the parking lot, confident her prayer would be answered.

CHAPTER 7

Luke Jones put the empty glass on the bar. "Hey, Al," he shouted as he bounced the glass off the over-shellacked surface. Luke had been coming to Al's Place since he had gotten out of jail, but only when he had money, since Al shut him off whenever he learned that Luke had lost another job. But today, Luke was loaded, and impatient. "Al, you're losin' money over here and I'm getting sober."

"Don't get uppity, reject." Pushing 300 pounds on a five-foot-eight-inch frame, Al rumbled out of the bathroom and walked behind the bar. On the way through, he closed the hinged counter top. He grabbed the Black Velvet from the shelf with his chubby fingers and poured a shot into Luke's glass. "Who'd you rob, anyway?"

Luke glared at the fat Latino man, "How come everybody thinks I robbed somebody?"

Al raised his eyebrows at Luke and busied himself cleaning the glasses in the deep-well sink. In the late sixties when this neighborhood bar had first opened, it had been quite pleasant. Now it was a dive. Al kept his joint as neat as he kept himself: not very.

The original wood floors had been covered with linoleum at the turn of the twenty-first century. The 'Millennium upgrade' Al called it. Now the floor was cracking, especially in front of the corner door. The tables and chairs were made with steel bases. Torn, fake leather cushions were on the chairs, and the wooden Formica table tops were adorned with cigarette burns and scratches. Each of the four small windows in the two paneled exterior walls had a neon sign. The only one that still worked was an OPEN sign that glowed red and blue. Al had purchased it from Sam's Club over two years ago in an attempt to let would-be patrons know that the building was not condemned.

Luke faced the bar and didn't bother to look up from his drink when the door creaked open. Al did. When he recognized Tony and Raymond, he grabbed a nearby overflowing garbage can and disappeared through the kitchen door. Raymond stopped and glared at two men who sat at the corner table. The men looked at each other, emptied their glasses, and calmly but quickly walked out the door.

Tony approached the bar and leaned into it. Startled, Luke twisted, surprised to see the scarred face of his old friend staring at him.

"Tony! What the hell happened to your face, dude?" Luke laughed and imagined that he was quite the clever jokester.

"That joke was old five years ago, Luke."

"Still makes me laugh every time. How you doin', man?"

Tony's eyes tracked Raymond, who planted himself behind Luke. "Better than you, Luke…better than you."

Luke stopped laughing when he sensed the person behind him. He pleaded with Tony, "Please tell me that isn't that meathead Raymond standing behind me." Instantly, Luke realized that he could have chosen better words.

At warp speed, somehow managing to miss the glass of whiskey, Raymond clutched a handful of Luke's unruly hair and introduced Luke's face to the bar.

Luke screamed and quickly stuck two fingers from his left hand up his nostrils to stem the river of blood that instantly streamed out of his nose.

"Jesus is not pleased with your repayment plan." Raymond released his grip on Luke's hair and took hold of Luke's right arm, twisting it behind his back.

Tony yanked a couple of bar napkins out of the cheap plastic holder on the bar and threw them at Luke. Grateful, Luke pulled his fingers out of his nose and snatched the napkins. He gently covered his bleeding proboscis.

"I've got money for you." Luke managed to squeak out.

"Bullshit!" Raymond said.

"Come on, Raymond, let him go," Tony ventured, "he said he's got money. Besides, Jesus said he didn't want anything broken today."

"Oops," replied Raymond. He released Luke's arm and grinned. "I might have broken his nose."

"Today?" cried Luke. "What do you mean, today?"

"He means if you don't come up with the grand you borrowed from Jesus, you're gonna need a wheelchair to get around." Raymond enjoyed his work. His grin kept getting bigger as he continued, "Then your old buddy, Tony, gets to do the deed. Don'tcha, Tony?"

Luke turned to Tony. "I only borrowed five hundred. I gotta pay back six. What does he mean a grand?" Luke switched the napkin into his right hand and reached into his left sock and dug out the hundred-dollar bill he had stuffed there this morning. "I got a hundred, right now."

"Then you only owe nine hundred." Raymond reached around and snatched the bill from Luke's hand.

"Hey, Raymond, ratchet it down a few notches, will you?" Tony glared at him.

"Piss off," was the big man's response. He glared right back at Tony and stuffed the bill into his pants pocket while he headed for the door. "Tell him." He barked his last command and walked out of the bar.

"Tell me what? Tony? Come on, nine hundred dollars?—I just lost my job!"

"You borrowed the money two months ago, Luke. The hundred dollars interest was for the first month. The rest is interest for the second month, plus late fees."

Luke pleaded. "Where am I gonna come up with nine hundred dollars? I don't know if I can come up with the five hundred. Tony, please man, come on."

"You did this, Luke, not me!" Tony yelled. "You got two weeks. Two weeks or I gotta bust you up, get it? Jesus is dead serious about this, so don't screw it up." Tony spun around and strode for the exit.

Luke jumped off the bar stool and lunged at Tony. He pulled Tony's arm and turned him around. "You and me were friends, damn it!"

Tony ripped his arm away from Luke's grasp and brought his face in close. "Ancient history, Luke." He took a step back and saw a bright crimson spot on his sleeve, "Dammit, you got blood on my shirt. A hundred bucks down the toilet."

"You paid a hundred bucks for one shirt?" Luke was incredulous.

Tony stormed to the door and looked over his shoulder. "Two weeks, Luke." He opened the door and left.

Luke stumbled over to his seat and collapsed onto the stool. He dabbed his nose and ripped off two pieces from the clean end of the paper napkin. He rolled them up and stuffed the pair into his nostrils just as Al came back through the kitchen door.

"Thanks for the warning, Al."

"What are you talking about? I had to take out the trash." Al eyeballed the mess that was Luke's nose and tossed him a rag out of the sink. "You better clean up that mess you made all over my bar."

Grabbing the rag, Luke began to wipe up the blood. Then, picking up the glass, he slurped the fiery liquid in one gulp. *At least they didn't search me,* he thought. Reaching into his right pants pocket, he pulled out a ten-dollar bill and smiled.

CHAPTER 8

Reverend James sat in the second pew of his chapel and stared at the cross—the cross he had come to love as a boy. Hundreds of stories were written down in the Matthews family journals, thousands of pages, dating back to his great-grandfather. Many were dedicated to what that cross meant to his bloodline; most were written by hand.

How did it come to this? The preacher shifted in the pew, the turmoil growing in his mind and heart, making him restless. He had never known emptiness like he felt today; like the glue inside of him that kept everything in its proper place was gone. Just—gone.

He covered his eyes with his hands and took a long deep breath. He exhaled and brought his hands down. Each time he looked the cross, it seemed to get slightly larger. Reverend James tried to look away from the cross but found he could not. Just when he felt like his mind was about to explode, the chapel door was opened.

Treena Williams, an overweight black woman of thirty-four, bustled into the room. She trundled across the floor and plopped herself down next to the startled preacher, blocking his exit with her large body. Treena had been at the hospital with her grandmother all night and most of the day and had totally forgotten about John Matthews' funeral. She might have received a clue if she had noticed the look on the preacher's face.

Treena's mind was totally wrapped up in an argument she had just had. She had come to find Reverend James to seek his advice. "Oh, Reverend, I'm so glad I found you. We really must talk."

Reverend James stared at her.

"It's about my son."

Reverend James' body went rigid, and his eyes began to flutter.

"I tell you, Reverend; it seems all that boy and I can do lately is argue. Why, just today when I got home from the hospital, he said to me..." Treena droned on, unaware of anything but the story she was sharing.

Reverend James' mind was elsewhere. It slipped into the memory of the morning Thelma had been killed, eight years earlier.

***

Thelma was putting the last of the dishes into the dishwasher. The eat-in kitchen was small, and the white appliances dated. There was a plate of eggs, bacon, and toast sitting on one end of the rectangular maple table that sat against the exterior wall. The four chairs around it were hard rock maple as well. A door that led to the basement was tucked into the corner of the room; an exterior door leading to the driveway was on the adjacent wall next to the table.

The sun streamed through the window above the single-basin stainless steel sink, highlighting the leaded glass cross that was hanging in its center. The ample white cupboards hung on the three walls away from the table. In the open spaces on the walls hung various framed proverbs. Cherished collectibles from previous generations were tucked neatly into the available counter space.

Thelma walked to the bottom of the stairs that emptied into the space from the adjacent hall and hollered up, "John Matthews, you are going to make us late for chur…."

Thelma stopped in mid-sentence when the thirteen-year-old boy bounded down the stairs and breezed out of the hallway and into the kitchen. He wore faded jeans and no shirt. His tall, lean ebony body gleamed with health. He walked across the floor, his ankle socks sliding on the hardwood, and opened the fridge.

"Do you know many times I had to holler up those stairs before I got to see that handsome face?" Thelma said to the refrigerator door.

"Aw, c'mon, Mom." John shut the door and carried the orange juice carton to the kitchen table and set it down next to his plate. He headed for the cupboard for a juice glass.

"You need to hurry up and eat your breakfast and get dressed for church."

"I'm not going to church today, Momma." John carried his glass back to the table and sat down in the chair.

Thelma put her hands on her hips. "I beg your pardon."

John stared at his glass while he filled it with orange juice. "I…I said—I'm not going to church today. All my friends are going to play basketball before tryouts. I'm going, too."

Thelma drew herself up. "And I said, 'I beg your pardon!'"

"I'll go next week." John pulled his breakfast closer and picked up his fork. He was about to dig in when the plate disappeared from view. He looked up to see his plate in his mother's hand. "Mom! I'm hungry!!"

Thelma walked over to the trash can in the corner, opened it, and dumped in his breakfast.

"Mom!"

Thelma's voice echoed off the walls. "Don't you, '*Mom, I'm hungry*' me, child. You get your butt out of my chair and get those feet moving up those stairs and get dressed for church."

Reverend James appeared in the hallway entrance to the kitchen. The wry smile on his face revealed he had listened to the altercation. "Is there a problem in here?"

"You just keep your nose out of this, James; this is between me and *your* son."

John Matthews rose from the chair. He knew he was outnumbered by much more than two to one. "Dad, I…"

"Move it, child," Thelma interrupted, "if you ever want to eat breakfast in my house again!"

John hesitated, and heard about it.

"MOVE!"

John dashed for the hallway and the stairs. He disappeared behind his father, who had lost the fight to keep in the laughter.

Thelma charged her husband and stood toe-to-toe. "Don't you be laughing at me, James. All he and I do anymore is argue."

"I'm not laughing at you, Thelma. I'm laughing at the look on John's face." The preacher wrapped his arms around her body and pulled her in close, his eyes sparkling with love.

Thelma feigned an attempt to break free from the loving embrace. "James, stop it." Gently, she bumped his arms and tried to push him away.

He was enveloped by her beautiful brown eyes and his voice deepened. "I love you, Thelma Matthews."

Thelma softened and blinked her eyes. Her sultry voice revealed the depth of her love. "Reverend James!"

***

Reverend James became aware of his left arm being poked, and his mind refocused on the present. He found himself sitting in the chapel with Treena Williams. She tried to get his attention and prodded his arm. "Reverend James? Reverend James?"

The preacher was still a little foggy. "Huh?"

"Are you even listening to me?" Treena asked.

"I'm sorry, Treena, no—I mean, yes..." The exhausted preacher struggled.

"I mean, I don't want to take up too much of your time," she continued. "Lord knows I don't get to church often enough."

"No, Treena, it's fine, it's just—it's been a really long day for me."

"I know what you mean, Reverend. I said to my son, 'Why do we always have to fight? What would you do without me?' Yes sir, Reverend, that's what I said to that boy. I said, 'Listen up, child. If the good Lord was to come a-callin' today and take me away from you, then you'd appreciate me. Only trouble is, it would be too late. Your momma'd be gone...'"

Reverend James' hearing faded away as Treena droned on. His consciousness was again lost to the memory of another day...

***

John and James Matthews were wrapped in each other's arms. The tears flowed as they stood in front of a large gravestone. It read:

THELMA MATTHEWS
LOVING WIFE AND MOTHER
Born: March 31, 1964
Died: June 24, 2007

John pulled his head off his father's chest and looked into his eyes. "It's not fair, Dad. We were fighting. The last thing she'll remember up in heaven is us fighting. I didn't mean to fight with Mom all the time. I mean…I didn't know that she would…she'd be…" He fell back into his father's arms and the tears flowed harder. He choked and gasped and hung on tight. "It's not fair, Dad. Why did God take her from us?"

Reverend James wrapped his arms even tighter around his son and his eyes went cold. There were no tears. He just stared at the block of granite. "I don't know, son. I truly don't."

John continued, "Maybe if I wasn't in such a hurry. Maybe if I hadn't wanted to go to basketball tryouts—"

"John!" The preacher stopped his son in mid-sentence. He pulled away and looked into John's eyes, gently holding his shoulders. "Blaming yourself won't bring her back, son." Tears crept into the preacher's eyes. The father and son shared the quiet, painful moment.

John looked at the gravestone again and wiped the tears from his eyes. "Dad," he threw his shoulders back, "I want to be a preacher."

On any other day that statement would have brought unbridled joy to Reverend James, an answer to dreams that had begun the day John was born…but not today. "That won't bring her back either, John."

"She would like that."

"You're right. Your mother would be very proud. So would I." He dropped his hands from John's shoulders. "I have always prayed that you would be called to be the fifth in a line of Matthews preachers.

We both prayed for that. But, you can't serve the Lord for me, and you can't do it for the sake of past generations, either." The preacher's voice became a whisper. "You shouldn't do it to serve the memory of your mother, either. You do it for the love of God."

"I do love God! I see the joy that you bring to people every day. I could do that, Dad. I know I could!"

"I know you could, too, believe me, John, I would love to see it, but I've also seen the way you tear up a basketball court when you play." Reverend James fought his desires and forced himself to focus on what he knew was best for his child. "You have a gift for basketball, John, a real gift. Your only shot to find out how far you can go with that gift is to try while you're young."

His father's passion transfixed John. "I didn't know you thought that. I mean, about basketball. Do you really mean it?"

The preacher forced a smile to his lips. "I really mean it. With hard work, who knows? You could go all the way."

John thought about his dreams of the NBA and smiled. Just as fast as the smile had appeared, it disappeared, and he became horrified as a new thought passed through his head. His eyes showed the fear.

"What is it, John? What's the matter?" Reverend James had seen the moment of happiness fade.

"Dad?" John crumpled into his father's arms, and Reverend James held him tight.

"What, John? What is it?"

Desperately, the young man clutched his father. "Please don't die!"

Clinging to his son, Reverend James wept.

***

Treena Williams sat in the second pew of the little chapel and rambled on. She turned to the preacher and found tears rolling down his cheek. "Reverend? There was no answer. "Reverend James?"

Reverend James no longer realized that Treena was sitting next to him. His eyes were fixed on the wooden cross that hung on the front wall of the chapel. Deep within the preacher something had snapped. He had lost his wife. He had lost his son. And now, he had lost himself.

He talked to the cross. "My—my son."

"What?" Treena asked.

Reverend James' voice grew in strength and intensity. "My son!"

Treena jumped to her feet, her eyeballs wide as she made the connection, "Dear Lord, I forgot! You buried your son today!" Treena backed out of the pew and explained as she went, "I was at the hospital with my grandmother…I'm so sorry." She turned and ran out the chapel door.

Reverend James continued to stare at the cross, oblivious to the fact that Treena had ever been in the room. The small leak in the dam of emotion that Reverend James had been fighting to keep in place became a rapidly-growing crack. He rose from his seat and his hands began to shake visibly. He stepped out of the pew, never taking his eyes off the cross. His tears slowed, and his anger grew. "Why him?" He took a step toward the cross.

He brought his shaking hands to his face, wiped his eyes, and tried to focus. He blamed his blurred vision on the tears that had been pouring out of his eyes. He wiped them again and still could not seem to clear the blur from his tormented mind. His head pounded with the fury of a thousand angry thoughts; his throat was dry like June in the desert. The cross loomed large across the altar. The preacher bore into it with eyes red with strain and grief. "You took Thelma from me," he croaked. "Wasn't that enough for you?"

Reverend James attempted to step up on the altar, a mere four inches above the floor where he now stood. The trembling that was in his hands had spread to his legs; the tip of his shoe suddenly caught the overhang of the step and spilled the broken man forward and down. He reached for the corner of the wooden table that sat in front of the cross, but the quaking arms would not respond and missed their mark. The preacher's forehead punched the corner of the table and split open. He crumpled to the floor, blinded by the pain and the blood that flowed into his eyes and down his face.

He shook his head and instantly regretted it. Pain ricocheted from his forehead to his eyeballs and back again. The expanding crack in the dam of emotion burst, and the preacher's body shook with rage. Through bloody and bleary eyes, he tried to focus on the cross, and his voice boomed like the crash of storm-driven waves upon the rocks. "Why did you take them from me?" Reverend James pounded his fist into the floor to emphasize his point as he screamed. "Why? Why? Why? Why, Why, Why—WHYYYYYYY??!!!!

The preacher leaped to his feet and flipped the table in front of him high into the air, and it crashed into the corner, shattering as it landed. Blood spattered the ceiling as the force of his movement sent it flying in all directions. Now it was just the preacher and the cross. He shook his fist at the wooden figure and screeched. "GOD DAMN YOU, WHY?!!"

The preacher assaulted the cross with his fists. He ignored the pain and the blood that painted the cross and wall. He punched one hole into the plasterboard next to the sculpted wood, and then another. He clawed at the wall and tried to get his fingers behind the wooden sculpture to tear it from its resting place. Chunks of crimson-stained plasterboard flew up and over his head. The hole around the cross widened, and he forced his fingers underneath the thick wood and pulled with frenzied force and unnatural strength; the pain and the passion combined to unleash the blazing torrent of anguish.

The wood loosened and its bolts snapped under the unrelenting attack. Reverend James grabbed the wood with both hands and yanked hard. Tearing the cross free from the wall, the preacher swung it high over his head like a pickaxe. It nearly bumped the ceiling and began its descent toward the floor.

The Healing of Reverend James

The memories of Thelma's crushed skull and John's withered, cancer-ridden body rampaged through his brain. Reverend James released a horrific scream and drove the arm of the cross into the floor with a super-human force he had never known before.

A crack of thunder exploded in the chapel, and a bolt of white light shot out of the cross where it split open, knocking the preacher backward, off the altar. He fell against the first pew.

Reverend James saw only white light and heard no sound. He panicked, choking on his breath; certain he was both blind and deaf. He pulled his knees under him and felt a strange calm permeate his mind.

The white light that had filled the room seemed to shrink. The walls of the chapel came into view, and the light consolidated itself over the top of the broken cross.

The preacher had a sense of lightness, and his pain dimmed.

The light gently swirled and faded, then grew brighter again and began to take shape. The shape of a person now floated over the broken cross.

Reverend James tried to move, but his body would not respond. He tried to think, but his mind was unresponsive as well. The calm that enveloped him removed the worry from his thoughts. With his mind at peace, he was finally able to think, and realized what had happened. *I'm dead,* the preacher thought. *I must be dead.* It was strange that there was no fear accompanying the thought of his death. He half-sat, half-knelt, and waited.

Reverend James Matthews.

Reverend James thought he heard his name coming from the light that floated over the cross. He stared at the floating figure, and it morphed before his eyes. This time it changed into a person he recognized. He knew of only two photos of this relative, but there was no mistake. Here, in the chapel he built over a hundred twenty-five years ago, floated the legless vision of his great-grandfather, Carlton Amos Matthews.

Reverend James Matthews.

There it was again. The sound was in his head like the shadow was talking to him without any noticeable movement. The preacher willed his mind to focus on the shadowy form. It looked like a hazy statue of his great-grandfather, white and transparent, yet blue and opaque. He focused on the face. Long hair that was pulled up and back, ending just above the shoulders. A strong chin and nose that he recognized as prevalent in his own photos, and a broad forehead with deep-set eyes that completed the picture. Reverend James gasped as the eyes, which had been closed, popped open. These were not the eyes that he had seen in the pictures. These eyes drew him into their endless depth, the fluorescent, blue-white pupils surrounded by the whitest white he had ever seen.

The preacher felt his body go numb until he could feel it no more. He joined the figure and floated above the floor, connected and apart, a disparity he could not reconcile with reality. Then he heard the voice again;

The Healing of Reverend James

Reverend James Matthews, your cries have been heard. Even with your faith, it appears life has broken you. You feel that you should be the one to stand in judgment of who lives and who dies. It shall be so. From this moment forth, your hands may heal the living, but not the dead. There will be much for you to learn, as the ability you now possess comes with three conditions you must discover for yourself. Learn well, Reverend James Matthews, learn well.

The eyes began to fade from view, and he could feel his body once more. The figure of his great-grandfather dissipated and swirled, and the light expanded to fill the chapel once more. Around and around the light spun and grew like a tornado that formed in front of the preacher's eyes. He felt nauseous and dizzy. The spinning light seemed to encircle him. He thought he saw the cross and the wooden table fly by him, and the light began to dim. He moved through the air and started to spin around the room. Faster and faster he went around the room as the light faded like footage of a sunset shot with a high-speed camera. Suddenly there was a mighty crash; the spinning stopped…and everything went dark.

CHAPTER 9

Reverend James heard a far-off drumbeat, a steady boom, boom, boom. He had always imagined harps or violins in heaven, but drums? He listened again, and the sound changed, like someone was hitting a can with a stick. A moment later, the pitch began to climb, and then he heard a beep, beep, beep. *I've heard that sound somewhere before,* he thought. S*omething was familiar about it, it sounded like—a hospital!*

The preacher opened his eyes and looked into a fuzzy white light. For a moment, he waited for the room to start spinning, but it did not. He continued to look into the light, and his eyes focused. A two-by-four-foot fluorescent light that was part of the ceiling above him came into view. He saw the familiar aluminum curtain rail that held the privacy curtain. He had been in many hospital rooms over the years. What did private mean, anyway? The only times these rooms were private was when nobody was in the other bed and the door was shut.

He followed the beeping sound down to the machine to the right of his bed. He read the monitor, 120/78. *Perfect,* he thought, *a dead guy with excellent blood pressure.* When he looked up at the IV bag hanging from the stainless steel hook, he abruptly realized he might not be dead. He became aware of pain radiating from his forehead and brought his hand up and felt the bandage there.

He was covered with a sheet and a light blanket. He lifted his eyes and flowers came into view—lots of flowers. He marveled at the amount of flowers that had been tucked and stacked onto the ledge of the window. along with three balloons that stated; GET WELL SOON.

He looked to his left and found no door, which meant he was in the back half of the room. He found three chairs along the wall and one of them was occupied. He recognized the occupant. "Patrick?"

Father Kirk jumped as he heard his name, and opened his eyes. He wiped his eyes and stood up and stepped over to the bed. "James, you're awake." He reached for the preacher's hand, and Reverend James grasped it and held on. "How are you feeling, James?" The priest continued.

The preacher attempted to sit up, shook his head, and tried to clear the cobwebs. The pain rebounded through his head and into his teeth. Letting go of Patrick's hand, he fell back into the pillow.

"You need to be careful, James. I better get your nurse." The priest started to walk away but stopped when he heard the panic in his friend's voice.

"Stay with me, Patrick."

The priest came back to the bed and placed his hand on the preacher's chest. "I really should get your doctor, James; you've had a pretty bad—"

"I thought I was dead, Patrick. I thought I was dead."

"You nearly did die, James. That was a nasty bump you took on your forehead. That's why I need to get your nur—." The priest saw the anguished look on Reverend James' face.

The memories of the chapel flooded back into the preacher's brain. Wide-eyed and filled with remorse, he tried to explain. "I lost control, Patrick. I didn't mean to break the cross—well, I guess I did mean to, but I was angry—."

"What are you talking about, James?"

"I'm talking about the chapel. What do you mean, what am I talking about?"

"You said you didn't mean to break the cross. Do you mean the cross in the chapel? That cross isn't broken." Father Kirk explained. "You hit your head on the corner of the table."

"The cross isn't broken? No, I remember, I ripped it off the wall and broke it." Reverend James was frantic. "Didn't they tell you about the chapel?"

"James, calm down, there's nothing wrong with the chapel." Extremely concerned, Father Kirk headed for the door. "I'm getting your nurse."

"Patrick, please! Don't leave."

The priest came back to the side of the bed and leaned in close. "I was in your chapel after you fell, James. There was nothing wrong with the cross." He stared into the preacher's eyes to emphasize the point. "Now, you stay calm, and I'll be back with your nurse right away." The priest moved quickly to avoid any further argument. He disappeared around the curtain.

Reverend James looked past the half-open curtain and through the windows into the sky. *I'm sure I broke the cross,* he thought. He was remembering his mother talking with him in the chapel just before all that happened. and suddenly, she was standing in front of him.

"Momma?"

A very concerned Mary Matthews smiled and spoke in a soothing tone, "James, how are you feeling, honey?"

Now he knew he was in trouble. His mother hadn't called him *honey* since kindergarten. "At the moment, I'm not sure, Momma."

"Well, that's okay, honey. We're just glad to have you awake." Mary reached down and patted him on the arm.

"Glad I'm awake? How long have I been here?"

"Don't worry about that, James. Reverend Washington said he can stay as long as we need him to. You just try to get some rest."

"Reverend Washington?" Reverend Washington only came down from Buffalo when he was on vacation, or seriously ill. That had only been three times in the last five years. "How long has Reverend Washington been here?"

"Three days."

"Three days!"

"He arrived Sunday morning and covered the services and the home visits after. He helped with the food bank yesterday and did some hospital visits today." Mary continued, "He was here earlier, but you weren't awake yet."

Reverend James closed his eyes and grimaced. The whole congregation knew. But what did they know? He wasn't even sure what was going on, yet. He needed to find out. "Momma, have you been to the chapel since our talk after—after John's funeral?"

"Yes. Patrick and I went to see where you fell. You're lucky Maya found you when she did."

"Maya found me?"

"Yes. Treena Williams called her when she got home. She was worried about you, and since Maya lives right on the corner, she came to check on you." Mary watched her son closely. "Treena told Maya you were weeping when she left."

The memories flooded back into the preacher's head. Treena had talked about her son, and something inside had snapped. Then he had tripped on the altar. "I saw Great-Grandfather Carlton."

Mary raised one eyebrow in dubious acknowledgment.

"Well, most of him, anyway. He didn't have any legs and he was floating over his cross that I had torn off the wall, and he looked at me with these blue and white eyes—."

"James!"

The preacher stopped at his mother's outburst.

"You hit your head, James…hard. You've been asleep for three days, and you just woke up, and I need to find…" She stopped in mid-sentence as Father Kirk entered the room with a nurse and doctor in tow.

"Thank the Lord." Mary sat in one of the three chairs along the wall to make room for the doctor to pass. Father Kirk planted himself next to her.

The doctor was tall, thin, and pretty. She had performed the usual battery of tests that followed a head injury. Concussion Protocol, it was called. Reverend James remembered the times he had gotten hit in the head as a child. His friends had laughed and joked about the *box of rocks* in his head. A man just sucked it up in those days. Not anymore.

"I'm going to schedule you for another CT scan later today, Reverend James." The doctor continued, "I'll look at it tomorrow, and if nothing changes and you're still doing as well as you are now, we'll see about releasing you." The brunette turned to Mary, "That was a nasty fall, Mrs. Matthews. Your son was very fortunate."

"Thank you, Doctor. Thank you, very much." Mary rose and was going to shake the doctor's hand, but seeing that it was formed into a fist; she curled her hand and gave her a bump. The doctor smiled and left, and the silent nurse followed.

The priest's and Mary's eyes met; in unison they turned to face the bed and Reverend James. It was quiet for just a moment. Mary opened her mouth, but was interrupted before she could speak.

"Would you both, please, just listen?"

Father Kirk and Mary sat as Reverend James addressed the proverbial elephant in the room. "I've told you both I broke the cross, and I told *you*, Momma, that I saw Great-Granddaddy Carton."

Mary started to rise. "James, now probably isn't the best…"

"Mother, please, sit."

She did.

"I'm not sure what happened to me, but I need to tell you what happened, because it's all I can think about." Reverend James paused. Father Kirk and Mary waited, so he continued. "I saw a legless figure that looked just like Great-Grandfather, and he said—or, rather, I heard in my mind—that I was given the gift of healing."

Mary and the priest shot a quick glance to each other but said nothing.

"And, the voice in my head said there would be three conditions on this gift that I would have to figure out for myself." The preacher looked at the pair and waited.

Nothing.

He continued, "It seemed very real to me, in an altered-reality kind of way."

"Listen to yourself, James," Mary answered. "It seemed real in a—in an altered-reality way? Oh James, you hit your head, honey."

There was that word again!

Father Kirk rose from his seat, "I think I'd best be going."

"Patrick?"

Father Kirk pasted a warm smile on his face. "It is obvious to me, James, that it felt real to you. I told you I saw the cross was unbroken. I just think I will leave you with your mother to talk about this. Too many cooks spoil the broth, right?" It was a lame answer, and Patrick knew it. Still, this conversation was silly. Of course, he wouldn't say it like that to his friend.

"I'll see you when you get back and get settled, James. Goodbye, Mary."

"Thank you for everything, Patrick, you are a dear friend." Mary kissed the priest on the cheek, and he was gone.

"He thinks I'm crazy," Reverend James said.

"He thinks nothing of the sort. Now, honey, why don't you try to get some sleep?"

"I just slept for three days, Momma."

"Maybe you woke up a little too early."

Reverend James was surprised by his mother's sarcasm. "Mom, do you have to treat me like that? You never make fun of people. Now you're calling me honey and being sarcastic."

Mary stepped in closer to her son and clasped his hand. "You're right, James. I'm sorry for upsetting you."

"Thank you."

"But we're on new ground here."

The preacher cocked his head to one side as he tried to determine where his mother was going with the conversation.

"I may never have been sarcastic before, but you have never seen spirits before, either!" Mary put her hands on her hips. "Which one of us, do you think, is further out on a limb? You should hear yourself, child."

"Don't you think I know that?" The preacher squirmed in his bed, the frustration making him uncomfortable. "It just felt so real. I truly believe I ripped that cross off the wall and broke it."

"How could you possibly get that cross off that wall, James? Your daddy had the workmen attach it so it would never come off."

"I beat the wall apart with my fists and..." He stopped when he looked at his fists. Not a scratch. His eyes shot up to meet his mothers' eyes. "There was blood everywhere." His voice faded.

"Did this happen before you hit your head, or after?

Reverend James thought for a moment, and his hands fell to his chest. "After."

Mary tried to keep the patronizing smile off her face. "Now do you see why I'm struggling with this, honey?"

The preacher glared at her.

"I'm sorry, James. Do you understand now?"

Reverend James allowed the logic to sink in. He looked at his hands again and suddenly felt very tired. "Yes, Momma, I understand."

"We'll get through this, James, I promise. Right now, you need sleep." She pulled the blankets up and gently tucked him in. He closed his eyes and was asleep before she kissed him on his forehead.

CHAPTER 10

A few days later, Reverend James walked into the chapel. He traced his finger along the cross where he thought the crack should have been.

Nothing.

He retraced the line and still couldn't feel a bump or crack. No sign of any damage at all. *It seemed so real.* He took a step back to see if a change of perspective would reveal a line or crack.

Still nothing.

The preacher backed up some more and examined the table where he had smacked his head. The table didn't have any obvious damage, and there was just the faintest outline of a stain on the floor. *That's from my blood,* he thought. *Strange that I remember breaking that cross in half, just as well as smacking my head, but nothing's wrong with the cross.*

Reverend James just couldn't fathom it. It had been so real. It still felt like the memory of something that had actually happened. He walked to the cross again and pressed his face against the wall to get a side view. He backed up, sliding his face along the wall, then forward again.

"Do you have any idea how ridiculous you look, Reverend?" Maya Richards tried to hold the laughter in, but couldn't.

The preacher straightened up and tried to find a stance that would make him look less awkward than he felt. Judging by the look on Maya's face, the attempt was a total failure. He pasted a sheepish grin on his face.

Maya walked over and stepped up on the altar. She surprised him by wrapping her arms around him and nestling her head just under his chin. When she wouldn't let go, he held her. It was then he recognized the tears.

"Maya! Are you crying?"

Maya pulled her head out from under his chin and looked him in the eye. "What makes you think that?" She smiled and tucked her face back under his chin and drew her arms tighter.

He had no idea what was going on but held on tight, anyway. He'd been a preacher too long not to recognize a person who needed to be held. On an impulse, he kissed her on the top of her head.

Maya didn't move, with the exception of the smile that spread across her face. "Thank you."

"For what?"

She pulled away, and he dropped his arms to his side. "For not pushing me away."

"Sure, Maya, anytime. I really appreciate you…"

He stopped when Maya swatted him on the arm, hard. There were still streaks on her cheeks where tears had been falling just seconds earlier. Her eyes were wide, and her hands were on her hips. Just like his mother, yesterday, and for the same reason, too. He was in trouble, and he didn't know why.

"What's that for?" he ventured.

"I about had a heart attack after Treena called, and I came in here and found you in a pool of blood. I thought you were dead!"

He opened his mouth to respond but didn't get a chance. Maya wasn't finished.

"It looked like a murder scene in here. I called 911 and held you until the ambulance got here. Then the police questioned me. Me! They wanted to know where I was when you supposedly fell."

Once again, he sucked in a breath but was stopped from speaking.

"Where was I? WHERE WAS I? Do you know what I told them?"

The preacher didn't even try.

"I was home attempting to make myself some dinner. That's what I told them." She stuck her finger into his chest. "I told them they better stop worrying about where I was, and they better get back to the station where they belong." Maya stopped poking him when she saw the smile starting to form on his face. "Are you laughing at me? This is serious. I thought you were dead!"

Reverend James tried to stop the spreading grin, but to no avail. The madder Maya got, the more he wanted to laugh. The bigger his smile got, the madder she got. Finally, he couldn't hold it back any longer and laughed and apologized at the same time. "I'm sorry, Maya, I'm not treating this lightly, really, I'm not. It all just seems like—like a very real dream."

Maya's anger turned to sorrow so fast the entire mood changed in a heartbeat. She looked him in the eyes, her own growing large and intense. "I thought you were dead." Maya left the stunned preacher staring at her back as she turned and bolted for the door.

She stopped at the door and turned back to him and hit him with a brick. "Thelma and I were best friends, James. I miss her more than words can say. Out of respect for her and John, I kept myself busy with the choir and the church for the last eight years."

He was totally confused now. The mention of Thelma and John in the same sentence didn't help. Something was different about Maya today. She had taken over the office management for the church when Thelma had passed, and had done a fabulous job. Now there was some kind of problem? Something was wrong. The preacher decided just to wait and see what the issue was. *Who can understand the inner workings of a woman's mind?* He thought. Years of sticking his foot in his mouth had revealed the secret. *When in doubt, shut up!*

"We've worked together for eight years," Maya continued, "eight years! I figured that someday you'd understand. Well, I was wrong."

Now he knew for sure he was in trouble. He wasn't sure what he had done, yet, but he knew he was about to find out. Why now? His son had just been buried a few days ago.

"This may be the worst timing ever, and I'm sorry for that." Maya started to cry again, the tears rolling down her cheek. "It's just that I saw you laying there," she looked down at the blood stain on the floor, "and I thought you were gone."

The Healing of Reverend James

There were so many thoughts that bounced around inside the preacher's head that he forgot his own hard-earned wisdom and spoke. "I'm okay, Maya. You don't need to worr—"

"Just for once, could you please shut up and listen?"

The preacher chastised himself for not following his own mantra, and clammed up immediately.

"This is hard enough for me to say without you making it harder." When Maya was sure the preacher wasn't going to interrupt, she tried again. "I've wanted to say this so many times, and, for one reason or another, the timing wasn't right." She looked him in the eye. "Maybe the timing will never be right."

Reverend James kept his mouth shut, and his eyes focused on Maya. *She's probably going to ask me for a raise.*

"Will you go out with me?"

He got a confused look on his face, his brain unable to make the connection between the words he had heard come out of Maya's mouth and any of the thoughts in his head. The moment he made the connection, his mouth fell open, and he looked at Maya in disbelief. He managed to get his mouth working.

"Out with you?"

"Yes."

A simple yes or no would have been sufficient. Currently, Reverend James was not capable of a thought process that would lead to either of those. "Out with you?" Repetition was the best he could come up with.

"Yes, Reverend, that is the question."

"Like—on a date?"

Maya started to cry again but kept her chin up. "I'm sorry, James. I knew this was awful timing. I just—I thought you were dead."

Reverend James snapped out of his mental stupor. The jumbled mess in his head cleared long enough for him to walk over to Maya and wrap her up in his arms. He just held her. Gently he rocked her back and forth to soothe her. Over the years, he had done the same for many in his congregation. This was different. He had shut his emotions down when Thelma died, choosing to spend any free time he had to focus on his son. Maya was beautiful and strong and reminded him of Thelma. He had thought of asking her out on many occasions. *The timing was never right, just like she said.* Maya felt good in his arms.

Maya pulled herself out of the embrace, knowing she had picked the wrong time and place. She wiped her tears with the back of her hand and tried to think of a clever way out of this mess. She didn't get the chance.

"Yes."

"Yes?" Now it was Maya's turn to struggle with the mental processing of simple information.

"Yes, I would like to go on a date with you." The preacher mustered a smile for her benefit. "I just need a couple of weeks to get my head together after—

after all this." He motioned to the cross and his forehead.

"I'm sorry, James. I—"

"Please don't be sorry, Maya. I've thought about asking you the same question many times over the last few years." His face sobered at the thought, "...the timing was never right."

Maya smiled. She liked the way he used her words to explain. "Well, then, you just let me know when—when you are ready. "

He reached out and took her hand in his. "We work together every day. Just a little time is all I need." He pulled her hand to his lips and gave it a gentle kiss, and let it go.

"Well, okay. I guess I'll get back over to the office and get the home visit list." She could still feel his lips on her hand, but Maya's mind calmed as she focused on the work to be done that day.

"Reverend Washington made a copy and marked up everybody he visited. If you think you're up to it?"

"I *need* to get back to work."

Maya nodded and went through the door. Reverend James followed but held the door open long enough to take another look at his great-grandfather's cross. It looked perfect. Lost in thought about his vision, he closed the chapel door.

CHAPTER 11

Reverend Matthews greeted the last of the parishioners who were headed home after the Sunday service. He closed the double doors and walked into the church. He glanced at the chapel door, his great-grandfather's cross visible through the glass, and thought about the last couple of weeks.

It had been two weeks and one day since he had buried his son. *Not that I'm counting.* He worked his way down the center aisle, consumed with thoughts of John. How many times had he given grief counseling to people who had lost children to disease, or worse, violence? Four dozen, maybe as many as fifty times, and he had never understood just how totally life changing and overwhelming this nightmare was. *Everything I see, everything I touch, reminds me of the times that John saw and touched those same things.*

Reverend James had decided that today he would pick a day for his first date with Maya. He needed to do something different. His house felt so empty. The quiet was unbearable: No basketball bouncing off the driveway. He missed the swish of a perfect free throw and the echo of the layup bouncing off the backboard, John's friends laughing and teasing him and each other when they came into the house and decimated the contents of the refrigerator. The last three years, seemingly endless trips up I-90 to Syracuse University, over three hours one way. That had become his life after Thelma. Now there was just the empty house and a full fridge, with no family. Yes, today was the day. He had to try to have a life.

The preacher stepped up on the altar and walked past the lectern. He headed for the door at the back of the altar, behind the choir risers, which led to the church offices.

In the many conversations he and Thelma had, they had always agreed if something should happen to the other, the surviving partner should move on with their life, whatever that meant. For the last eight years, that had meant devoting every waking moment to the church and their son. John had been away at college for the last three years, but home every summer. He was so happy they had had those conversations. *I never thought I would actually need to think of it like that,* he thought, *no one really plans on having to deal with something like that, do they?*

He opened the door and entered the five-foot-wide hallway. To his right was the music room with a piano and seats for thirty people, fewer if someone was afraid to be friendly. A closet along the north wall of the music room held the choir robes and music supplies.

To his left was his office. He walked in and went behind the desk and pulled open the second drawer. Pulling the cherished Bible out of his suit pocket, he gently placed it in the drawer. He sat in the faux leather chair and leaned back, taking a few minutes to let his mind wander over the events of the last two weeks.

The day he buried John had been awful. He remembered feeling anger like he had never felt before. Then it had spun out of control with the dream about breaking the cross in the chapel. A dream that had felt so real he still had trouble when he attempted to rationalize it as only a dream...his legless relative floating over the broken cross and telling him he could heal people. Four days in the hospital with Reverend Washington taking over for him. Then there was last Sunday, his first sermon after John's funeral. The whole congregation watched to see if he could keep it together. He did, barely, but never felt so awkward during a sermon since his first one over thirty years ago. This week had been better, but there was still the awkwardness, the loneliness, and the quiet.

The one bright spot in all of this was Maya. Somehow, in the middle of the nightmare that his life had become, she had picked the most awkward moment possible to ask him out. He felt hopeful. Well, confused at first, but now hopeful.

A stack of papers landed on his desk and snapped him out of his thoughts, and there she was, standing right in front of him. Maya looked good in her tasteful just-over-the-knee-length mint green skirt, antique white blouse, and matching jacket. She gave him a smile but was all business in her demeanor. She held a manila folder in her hands.

"That's the updated visitation list for today's visits," Maya began, "I added Regina Jablinski last. She got home from the hospital yesterday, in case you didn't know. She called me three times to make sure you were going to see her today."

"Why didn't she call me?"

"She did. Three times. Do you even have your cell phone on you? If you do, is it turned on?"

Reverend James checked his pocket and found it empty. He was always leaving his smartphone in any number of locations. He tried to move into the twenty-first century but felt too overwhelmed by the whole social media culture. Smartphones, texting, Facebook, Twitter, Instagram, and more: he just couldn't keep up with all that communication, so he didn't try.

"I must have left it at home."

The sheepish grin was wasted on Maya. "Uh-huh." She turned to walk out of the room but stopped when she heard his magical words.

"Would you like to have dinner with me Tuesday night?

Maya turned around and tried to keep the smile from knocking her ears off her head. "Yes, yes I would."

"This Tuesday?"

"This Tuesday, next Tuesday—come to think of it, I think my Tuesdays are available for the foreseeable future." Maya's eyes danced as she opened up the folder in her hand and dropped a sheet of paper onto his desk.

"What's this?" the preacher asked.

"My weekly schedule; as you can see, I've got Monday and Wednesday choir rehearsals, and I work here all week. Every other night and all day Saturday

I'm available." She enjoyed the look on his face too much.

The preacher laughed and returned the smile. "You always were prepared. Time?"

Maya looked at her watch. "Twelve forty-eight pm."

"No. I meant..." He stopped at the sound of her laughter and realized she had just been kidding.

"How about six o'clock?" Maya asked through the giggles. She was forty-nine but felt thirteen at the moment.

"I'll pick you up," he said.

Maya headed for the door and answered on the way out. "I'll see you then." She was gone.

The preacher put his hands behind his head and leaned back in his chair, savoring the brief moment of joy. Then he thought of John and the smile faded. He sighed and stood, picked up the papers from his desk, and walked out the door.

CHAPTER 12

Luke Jones stumbled out of the door of Al's Place. Slamming the door, he screamed, "A guy can't even get credit at his neighborhood bar anymore, what the hell!" Luke raised his middle fingers on both hands and waved goodbye to the bar. Staggering a few more steps down the street, he stopped. He twirled around, looking for his car, and found it parked in the middle of the parking lot, right where he had left it two hours earlier.

He reached into his pocket and pulled his keys out. On the way to the car door, the keys tumbled out of his hand, bounced off his feet, and landed under the car. Luke half crouched; half fell onto the broken pavement that was the parking lot. He lay on the asphalt and talked to the car, "I need a nap." A second later he shook his head and retrieved the car keys. He jumped to his feet and lost his balance, stopping his fall with his face against the car. Using one arm for balance, he aimed the key at the keyhole and found it on the third try. He opened the door, ignoring the creaks, and planted himself in the driver's seat.

The Caprice sputtered to life. Luke put the car in gear and started forward, but stopped when he realized the door was still open. He reached for the door and nearly tossed himself out onto the ground, but managed to spare a face plant when he caught the armrest at the last second. He pulled the groaning door shut.

Sunday afternoon, he thought, *that's a great time for a nap.* Putting the car in gear, he drove out onto the road and disappeared around the corner.

***

It was still early Sunday afternoon when Reverend James shouted through the open door of the modest house, "I'll stop by again on Wednesday night, Mrs. Jablinski." He closed the door tight and checked to see that it was locked. He put the key back under the ceramic flower pot next to the door and remembered a time when people didn't have to keep their doors locked. Too many people and not enough opportunity for a decent job led to all types of dysfunctional people. *I have to figure out a way to help more of our young people,* he thought.

There was the local YMCA for basketball, but you couldn't swim there anymore thanks to a wrongful death lawsuit. *Money, it always came down to money, didn't it?* Money had been an issue in every decision he'd ever been forced to make. He had been shocked by the thousands of dollars collected for the American Cancer Society at John's funeral. More than ten times the average collection amount. He knew that meant many people had given more than they could afford, a reflection of how much John meant to the community.

John had spent this past summer helping to remodel one of the local food banks that Father Kirk had started in an abandoned building next to his church in South Jamestown. The building had been a donation from a parishioner who had bought it at a tax sale. John had become too weak from the chemo to play basketball, so he had organized his friends to take up donations to put a new roof on the donated building.

When John had gotten too ill or tired, he would lie on a cot on the front porch while his friends and volunteers worked around him. With the new roof in place, they had talked to Home Depot and had received donations of enough materials to knock down walls and build more shelves. The remodeled food pantry had opened just two weeks before John had passed. Reverend James had promised John he would expand the small pantry of emergency food supplies in the basement of their church as well. He would be starting that work as soon as money allowed.

Reverend James refocused and looked at the list in his hand. He had visited everybody on the list Maya had given him. He didn't feel like going home to his empty house, and the weather was warm for late September, so he decided to make the three-quarter-mile hike down to Father Kirk's church. He remembered the cell phone in his pocket but decided against calling. If Patrick wasn't there, he would walk over to the pantry and stock whatever donations had been dropped on the porch.

He walked off Mrs. Jablinski's porch onto the sidewalk and headed south. He knew it was likely that Patrick was in his offices. In 1956, the house next door to the church, opposite the new pantry, had been purchased and converted into offices downstairs and living quarters for the priests upstairs. In the 1960s, there had been two priests for the Catholic congregation. Jamestown had been growing up to that point, but since Patrick had arrived, there had been only one priest and two secretaries who had to make everything work. *Money rears its ugly head again,* he thought. That was life.

The preacher inhaled deeply and made an effort to concentrate on enjoying the walk. The problem was everything around him sparked memories of his son. He looked at the trees and remembered the science project where they had gathered twenty-four species of tree and shrub leaves. It *had* to be two dozen, John had insisted. The other kids in class had brought in pictures, and information on the trees and shrubs gleaned from internet searches; anyone could have done that, but people could smell and touch John's leaves and branches. He received an A+ for his efforts.

Reverend James was remembering his first attempt at teaching John to ride a bike when he suddenly heard a noise behind him. He turned to see Tommy Hinkle rolling up the road on a skateboard.

"Out of the way, Preacher-man, comin' through!" shouted Tommy. He was covered in tattoos up both arms and down both legs. His nose ring sparkled as he rode past. Earbud wires dangled on top of the holes in his earlobes that were filled with guages, a newer type of jewelry that some of the kids were wearing. His shorts were barely hanging on his butt, and the t-shirt he wore was white and tight.

Reverend James waved when the youth rolled by. He didn't know him well, but he had helped with the roof of the food bank at Patrick's church. The preacher shouted after him, "Hey, how about a ride?" The question fell on deaf ears; the music coming through the earbuds was the only thing that the young skateboarder could hear. Reverend James remembered a time before the rise of X-games when skateboarding was much less accepted. He was thinking about John's short obsession with Tony Hawk when the scene in front of him jolted his mind into the moment.

Tommy was headed for the intersection just a few yards in front of his skateboard when his shorts slipped off his backside. He was so busy trying to pull them back up that he rolled right through the stop sign and didn't see and couldn't hear the car speeding toward him from the intersecting road.

The Chevy Caprice had no stop sign, and Reverend James knew it. He screamed at the top of his lungs, trying to alert the driver. "Watch out! STOP, STOP, STOP!" The preacher heard the squeal of car brakes, but it was too late. Tommy tried to stop but had become aware of his dilemma just seconds before the impact.

The preacher watched as the car struck Tommy in the legs and sent him flying and spinning into the air. The car was dented but continued through the intersection, the youth's weight not enough to slow it down. Reverend James watched Tommy hit the pavement with a thud and roll into the curb, his body lying face up, his legs broken and bleeding.

The Caprice came to a stop fifty feet past the intersection. The door opened, and Luke Jones half fell out of the car. Leaving the car door open, he jogged back through the intersection toward the person he had just run into. He had been adjusting the radio and had seen a figure in front of his car at the last moment.

Reverend James ran toward the boy as well and stopped in his tracks when he saw Luke. If the preacher could have described his worst nightmare, it would have looked something like what he saw before him at that moment. *Luke Jones! Of all the people in this city, it had to be Luke Jones.*

The explosion in the preacher's mind was pure and uncontrollable rage. He hurled his body at Luke and tackled him. The pair landed half on the asphalt and half on the grass in one corner of the intersection. The preacher rolled up on top of Luke, his hands around Luke's throat. With blind fury and memories of his dead wife burning through his brain, he choked the man, hoping he would die.

Luke grabbed the preacher's wrists and desperately tried to loosen the grip around his neck. His airway was almost totally cut off; he struggled for breath. He could not remove the stronger man's hands from his throat, so he thrashed and gouged at the preacher's eyes. His panic ascended to the plane of terror. He knew it would be only seconds until he passed out…then he heard a moan.

Tommy Hinkle woke up and groaned. When Reverend James heard the groan, he realized that Tommy was still alive, and he released his grip from Luke's throat. The air rushed into Luke's lungs, and he gagged and choked as the preacher rolled off him.

The Healing of Reverend James

Reverend James forced his shaking body to stand, and he stumbled toward Tommy. He fell halfway there and covered the remainder of the distance on all fours.

He looked down at the broken young man who was bleeding from his nose, mouth, and ears. Somewhere in the preacher's mind he heard a voice telling him to call 911, but his weakened and trembling body would not answer. He squatted on his haunches like a dog told to sit, and tried to make his body respond to help the broken young man in front of him. But all he could remember was his hand around Luke's throat, and the awful and wonderful thought that Luke would be dead soon.

He looked over at Luke, who had rolled onto his belly and was on all fours sucking in air. Their eyes met for a moment, and the preacher was filled with remorse for the joy he had felt at nearly killing the man. He couldn't get his mind to focus on the rampaging thoughts in his head. He was overwhelmed by his emotions and shook his head in a desperate attempt to make his brain work again.

Tommy groaned again.

I've got to call 911, the preacher thought. He knew this young man would be lucky to survive the injuries he saw in front of him, and wouldn't if he didn't act fast. Reverend James tried to thrust backward in an effort to sit up and get to his phone. His arms lifted off the ground, but his drained body could not keep him upright, and to his horror he fell forward, both hands landing on Tommy's chest.

As Reverend James fell on top of Tommy, a flash of light shot out of the preacher's hands and traced the broken body of Tommy. Tommy's body started to glow with a bright, fluorescent light, and then the light was sucked inward like water on a dry sponge. A split second later the light appeared to burst out of Tommy and disappear in every direction. Reverend James was temporarily blinded by the intense brightness of the light.

Just a second later, he looked at Tommy and gasped. The blood was gone, and Tommy's eyes were open and alert. Tommy's legs were straight, and both legs faced the same direction.

The youth looked startled to see the preacher's hands on top of his chest. Tommy swatted the preacher's hands off of him and jumped to his feet. He looked at Reverend James and then spotted Luke staring at him. Without a word, Tommy leaped up onto the sidewalk. He stopped when he spotted his skateboard lying in the grass. Running to it, he picked it up. The skateboard was broken in half, and one set of wheels was missing. Tommy looked at the two men again and then took off. Down the street he ran, in the direction he was heading before he'd been hit.

The preacher watched Tommy go, and then stared at his hands. He brought them up in front of his face and turned them back and forth, unable to reconcile what had just happened. His mouth was open and his breathing uneven. His hands fell onto his legs and exhaustion overwhelmed him. *It wasn't a dream!* The events in the chapel; the broken cross, his great-grandfather telling him he had the power to heal people! It was all real!

The preacher lifted his head up and looked around. *Where are all the people?* He looked in the other direction and stared into the eyes of Luke Jones. For a moment, the two men knelt in the corner of the intersection and stared at each other. Luke managed to stand up, feeling his neck. Reverend James saw the red and purple marks on Luke's neck and was stunned by the fact that *he* had done that to him. The same hands that just saved a life had nearly taken a life just seconds earlier. The preacher realized he owed Luke an apology. *Do I owe him an apology? He killed my wife!* He tried to stand and managed to get one foot flat on the ground. "Luke, I…"

Luke heard his name come out of the preacher's mouth, but his mind was blown. What he had just seen was impossible. The kid had been bleeding and mangled. He had seen it with his own eyes. The flash of light and, boom, like magic, he was fine. Luke wasn't sure how it had happened, but he was sure what to do about it—what he always did in times of extreme stress—run!

Luke ran for his car, grateful he had left the engine running and the door open. He jumped into the driver's seat, slammed the car door shut and rammed it into gear. The car lurched forward as Luke pushed the gas pedal all the way to the floor.

Reverend James wrestled with his muscles and tried to stand. He watched Luke jump into the car and speed away. His legs argued and cramped, but he insisted they move faster, and somehow they finally responded. He heard the squeal of brake pads and looked up and saw the Chevy stop in the middle of the road, about two hundred yards in front of him.

Luke's hands shook, and his head ached. He reached for the glove box door and dragged out an empty bottle of Black Velvet. "SHIT!" He screamed at the bottle and threw it onto the passenger seat beside him. He went into the compartment again a pulled out the photo of his three girls. "Jennifer." He said to the picture, suddenly feeling very alone.

Movement in the rear view mirror caught his eye and he looked out the back window and saw the preacher running toward him. "Damn!" He threw the picture on top of the bottle in the passenger seat and tromped on the gas pedal again.

Reverend James got just close enough to the car to slap his hands on the trunk as it sped away from him, "Luke! We have to talk about this!" He shouted at the retreating vehicle. He saw that Luke was not going to stop, so he gave up the chase. His legs felt like lead, his breathing labored. He turned around in the middle of the street and saw no one. The preacher walked to the sidewalk and took long, deep breaths. His mind tried to rationalize the fact that a boy had just been struck by a car, and not one person had come out of a house and no cars had passed by. It just didn't make sense. It was Sunday afternoon and professional football was on, but—no one?

The preacher knew he had to share what had just happened with someone, but whom? The answer popped into his head instantly. *Patrick!*

The decision made, he forced his aching and exhausted body back toward the intersection where he had just healed the boy, and headed south.

CHAPTER 13

Luke's Caprice roared into Jennifer Santiago's driveway, the horn blowing and tires sending dirt and pebbles flying through the air. The car squealed to a stop, facing the house, and the driver's door flew open. Luke put his foot out onto the dirt driveway and leaned on the horn again. He screamed as loud as he could, "Jennifer!"

The front door of the three-bedroom, one bath ranch house opened. Jennifer marched onto the porch and down the four stairs to the driveway. The house was small and neat with an asphalt-shingle roof that needed to be replaced. It looked the same as the other houses in this sloping neighborhood; the hillside cut out and leveled to accommodate lot space for each small property. Jennifer had moved here a year ago, just one block from her older daughter's school so she wouldn't need a car. Jasmine walked to school, and Jennifer stayed home with two-year-old Morgan.

Her mother came over to stay with the girls five nights a week. Jennifer walked a mile to the hospital where she was a nurse's aide. She had been on public assistance for three years after Luke had gone to jail but had gone through the welfare-to-work program and had gotten a job immediately. She had lived with her mother for the previous seven years to help establish a decent credit rating.

After starting her job, Jennifer pinched pennies and had saved enough money for the twenty percent down payment on this thirty-two-thousand-dollar property. Nothing ever came easily to Jennifer and this jerk she had fallen in love with when she was sixteen years old continued to make it harder.

She both hated and loved the way Luke's eyes traveled over her curves. She knew she looked good in her sandals, hot pink short shorts, and tight fitting, little white sun top.

"You could try knocking on the door, Luke, instead of scaring us and my neighbors half to death!" Jennifer strode right up to the opposite side of the open car door to get in his face.

"Jennifer, you're not going to believe this…"

Jennifer looked into the car and was furious when she saw the empty Black Velvet bottle that sat on the front seat, "You're drunk!" She stepped back and looked at him in disgust.

"No, you don't understand…"

Jennifer had been down this road way too many times before and no longer believed that the best defense was a good offense. The best defense was to not take any crap from Luke. "I understand, Luke. I understand I told you never to show up here drunk again!" Jennifer glared at him and turned around, heading for the stairs.

Luke jumped around the open car door and ran after her. He caught her at the bottom of the stairs and grabbed her hand, spinning her around. "I've got to tell you…" He stopped in mid-sentence as Jennifer slapped him hard across the face. Luke grabbed his nose, which Raymond had broken just two weeks earlier. The pain radiated through his head and brought tears to his eyes. He looked up and found Jennifer crying, also.

"I don't want to hear it because it isn't going to work this time, Luke!" She heard the screen door squeak open and saw Jasmine and Morgan walk out of the front door.

The girls were wearing shorts and cotton blouses. Jasmine's hair was jet black and straightened; Morgan's curly locks were in a ponytail. They were both barefoot. The girls stared at their father.

"Jasmine, Morgan, back in the house, now."

The girls continued to stare at Luke. Morgan was two and on a mission, "I wanna see my daddy."

"NOW!" Jennifer charged up the stairs and chased the girls back into the house and closed the door behind them. The girls didn't deserve this, and Jennifer knew it, but what could she do? She turned back to Luke. "Please leave."

Luke's words made her heart stop. "I hit a kid with my car."

Luke watched Jennifer put her hands on her hips.

"You don't believe me? Look." He pointed to the grille and hood.

Jennifer walked down the stairs, covering her mouth with her hands. She looked at the dented and broken grille, and the hood that was folded back a couple of inches. She grimaced at Luke, asking the question without saying a word.

"No, the kid is fine. Well—he wasn't fine, but he is now. I mean, I think he is." Luke cringed at his inability to make sense of the sentence. He could still feel the panic, the crunch, and see the arms and legs flying above his windshield. He shivered.

"What do you mean you *think* he is fine?" Jennifer put her hands on her hips again, and Luke knew he was getting closer to trouble with every word, but he had to tell her what happened, didn't he? He just wasn't sure where to start. He decided just to tell it like it was.

"Well, I was driving home from the bar and…"

"I knew you were drinking! I could smell it the moment you got here."

Luke waited to give Jennifer time to enjoy her comment about the obvious. "I was driving home from the bar, where I had been drinking." He shot her a look. "And I looked down to adjust the radio, 'cause they were playing this crappy love song." He recognized her clenched jaw and decided to leave out the fact that it was *their* song that was upsetting him: John Mayer's "Your Body is a Wonderland."

"Anyway, I felt something was wrong, —you know how I get those feelings, so I look up and slam on the brakes 'cause I see this kid, but it's too late and, WHAM!" Luke smacked his hands together to emphasize the moment of impact. "And this kid goes flying up over my windshield—arms and legs flying everywhere, and—and I come to a stop a little ways down the road and I hop out of the car." Luke paused to catch his breath.

"Did you kill him?" Jennifer's hands covered her mouth again.

"Just wait, Jennifer. We're not even to the really good part, yet."

Jennifer covered her eyes and her forehead, certain that even though she couldn't feel it yet, a migraine would be coming soon.

"So, I hop out of the car and there's Reverend James right in front of me."

"Reverend James!" Jennifer was shocked. "You mean *my* Reverend James—from the church? Like, the man whose wife you killed?" Her mouth hung open, and her hands floated above her head even though she could no longer feel them.

"Yes, but wait—he jumps on me and starts trying to choke me to death with his bare hands." He pulled the collar of his shirt back and Jennifer gasped when she saw the red and purple bruises around his neck. She covered her mouth with her hands again. "So, then this kid, the one that I hit, starts to moan and the preacher lets go of me. I'm lying there, gagging and choking and he stumbles over to the kid and—I mean, Jennifer, this kid was bleeding from everywhere and his legs were busted up—I get up on my knees and then, bam, there's this flash of light that comes out of the preacher's hands and goes through the kid's body and like, explodes, or something. I couldn't see for a minute and the next thing I know, the kid jumps up and runs away."

Jennifer's hands fell to her side. Her face got red, and she charged Luke, punching and slapping him with all her might. "You drunken son of a bitch!" she screamed. She kept flailing at him while he attempted to cover his head from her violent attack. "Damn you to hell, Luke Jones!"

Luke grabbed hold of her wrists; he was getting hurt. Jennifer struggled and tried to break free from his grasp. Unable to break free, she burst into tears.

"I had your children, Luke. When they were born, you didn't even come to the hospital," she cried, "I waited for you when you were in jail because you promised to sober up and marry me."

Luke released her arms.

Jennifer looked him in the eye; her tears slowed. "You were sober just long enough to get me pregnant again."

"Jennifer, everything I just told you is the truth…it all really happened. I swear it."

"Just like you swore to give up drinking?" Jennifer wiped the tears from her cheeks and walked toward the stairs of her house. She stopped at the bottom of the stairs and turned to him again. "The sad part through all of this is—when you were sober—you were a wonderful father."

Luke didn't know what to say, so he gestured to the dent in the front of his car.

Jennifer looked at the dent in the car and sighed. Her shoulders dropped. "Luke, go away. You are welcome to come see your daughters any time you are sober." She walked up the stairs and crossed the porch and opened the door. She turned back to him, pain in her eyes. "Show up here drunk again…I'll call the cops."

Luke just stood and watched the mother of his two children as she walked into her house and locked the door.

The Healing of Reverend James

CHAPTER 14

Father Patrick Kirk sat in one of two handsome maroon leather wing-back chairs behind a beautifully ornate mahogany desk. Next to him was his church superior, Bishop Walters. The two men stared across the desk at Reverend James. The preacher sat opposite the priests on the edge of another leather chair in the priest's study.

On the walls on both sides of the study were floor-to-ceiling bookcases with neatly bound volumes in organized rows. Behind the two priests was a library table with a sterling silver tray and four matching crystal wine glasses surrounding a beautiful crystal decanter. Above the library table was a painting: oil on canvas of Jesus of Nazareth, with his arms spread wide and a halo around his head, one of the thousands produced for the American Catholic Church. The room was deep and led to a door to the rest of the church offices.

The preacher waited for the two Catholics to absorb what he had told them.

Father Kirk spoke first. "You said, 'a flash of light?'"

"Yes, Patrick, a flash of light. His body seemed to absorb the light, and then light seemed to—seemed to…for lack of a better word, explode out of him. Then the blood was gone, his legs were fine, and he jumped up and ran away." Reverend James knew the men doubted his story. If he had been told the same thing, he would have doubted it, too. He had to try. The preacher

117

was not pleased that Bishop Walters had picked this day to drive down from the Buffalo diocese, but that was a fact he couldn't change.

Bishop Walters looked at Father Kirk and back to Reverend James. "Maybe I should have let you two speak in private."

"I know it's hard to believe, Bishop Walters, but it's true." He looked to Father Kirk for support and found only concern. "I healed that boy."

Father Kirk leaned forward in his chair and lowered his voice. "James, I've made Bishop Walters aware of all you've been through lately."

The Bishop leaned forward as well, "Including one rather, well, an *angelic vision*, shall we say? Something about your great-grandfather—a legless figure floating over a cross you say you broke?" The Bishop leaned back in his chair and folded his hands in his lap. He looked down his nose at the preacher and failed to keep the condescending tone from his voice. "I understand the cross was not, in fact, broken."

Reverend James heard the tone and saw the look on the Bishop's face. He sat up straighter in his chair. He knew the truth and was unshaken, "It was no dream. It was real. I did see my great-grandfather, and I did heal that boy."

Father Kirk held his breath, and Bishop Walters examined his fingernails. When the silence was perfectly uncomfortable, the Bishop ventured. "Forgive me, Reverend James, were there any witnesses to this—healing?"

"Well, just the driver of the car that hit the boy, Luke Jones."

The two priests looked as if they had done the ice bucket challenge; their eyes popped open along with their mouths. The only thing missing were the screams. Father Kirk couldn't stop himself from asking the obvious question. "You mean the man that killed your wife?"

"Yes."

If there had been an awkward silence in the room earlier, it paled in comparison to the quiet that filled the room now. The two priests exchanged silent looks.

Bishop Walters' eyebrow rose as an idea furrowed its way into his brow. "Patrick, is Susan Erikson still here?"

Patrick looked at the digital clock on the desk. "She's due to leave any minute."

"Would you check and bring her in here?"

Father Kirk stood up and took a step toward the door. He stopped when the realization formed in his brain. He turned to the Bishop. "Bishop, I'm not sure…"

The Bishop was ice cold. "Please."

The priest did not want to go, but the look on the Bishop's face propelled him out of the room. Reverend James knew something was wrong; he just didn't know what. He was about to find out.

He heard Father Kirk's voice echo down the hallway, though he couldn't make out the words. The Bishop and he waited in silence. Soon, there were footsteps in the hall. Patrick walked back into the room. "She's here. She agreed to join us in a minute." He stopped by the preacher's chair and spoke to Reverend James in a quiet voice. "You know Susan. Remember. She was in an automobile accident two years ago. She's been in a wheelchair ever since."

Reverend James shot a look at the Bishop. "Show and tell time, Bishop?"

"If you can do what you say you can do, it would certainly be a miracle for Susan, now, wouldn't it?" The Bishop returned the steely gaze.

Susan Erikson rolled into the room in her motorized wheelchair. Her lower body was strapped into the chair, with a blanket covering her legs and feet. She wore an oversized sweater and red-rimmed glasses. Her hair was swept straight down, close to her head, and curled in under her chin.

Father Kirk closed the door behind her and walked back to his seat.

Susan could sense the tension in the room the minute she rolled in. She looked around at the three men and decided she didn't feel like waiting. "Okay. Who's in trouble? Me or one of you?"

Reverend James and Father Kirk deferred to the Bishop, looking at him immediately. The Bishop sighed and explained, "Susan, this is a little awkward—you see—Reverend James here claims to have been endowed with the power to heal people. We were kind of wondering if you would—if you would like to…"

The Bishop was let off the hook by Susan, who grasped the idea immediately. "So you grabbed the nearest cripple to use as a guinea pig, right?" She looked around at the startled faces and laughed. "Don't look so surprised, gentlemen, I'm disabled, not brain dead." She gave them an irreverent smile. The men still could not find the words, so she took matters into her hands and spun toward the preacher. "So, you're a healer, huh?"

"I think so, Susan. Everything has been a bit confusing lately." Reverend James gave Susan a brief review of the events that took place in the chapel, and the healing of Tommy. He left out any mention of Luke Jones.

When he finished, Susan was shaking her head. "No offense, Reverend James, but I sorta wish I hadn't asked." She laughed nervously, patting her hands on the armrests of her wheelchair. "What the heck. I'll try almost anything once, and the good Lord knows I've tried everything else. What's the procedure?"

The preacher knelt beside Susan so he could look directly into her eyes. "I'm not sure there *is* a procedure. All I did was put both my hands on Tommy. I told you about the light?"

"Yes, yes you did." She sat back in the chair and tried to relax. Then a thought occurred to her. "Is this going to hurt?"

"I don't think so," the preacher responded. "I don't know for sure. Tommy was unconscious at the time, when I healed him."

Susan leaned back again and was ready. "Let's try it."

The room grew quiet enough for the proverbial pin to be heard. The preacher took a deep breath and let it out. He reached his arms out and held them over Susan's legs. The moment of truth had arrived, and the two priests leaned forward in their chairs. Reverend James eased his arms down and placed his hands on her legs.

Nothing.

The priests exchanged looks and Susan worked hard to keep her mouth shut.

Reverend James decided to try again, and he made the sign of the cross to his head, heart, and shoulders, as he had watched Patrick do so many times in the past. Then he laid his hands on Susan's legs again.

Still nothing.

Reverend James took his hands off Susan's legs. "I'm sorry, Susan, something is wrong."

"Yeah, something is wrong, alright," she shouted to the stunned preacher, "my legs don't work!"

Susan tried to laugh her way out of it, until she looked at the other three faces in the room that weren't smiling. She allowed her laughter to fade to nothing and pulled on the controls, backing the wheelchair up.

"Well, I guess you don't need me anymore. So, I'll be rollin' out of here." She traveled to a stop in front of the door that Father Kirk had run over to open. She looked at Reverend James. "Thanks for trying, Reverend. Goodnight, Bishop Walters, Father." She nodded at the two priests and rolled out the door.

The Healing of Reverend James

Reverend James' gaze met Father Kirk's. The priest shrugged his shoulders and couldn't think of anything to say.

Bishop Walters had no such trouble. "Well, Reverend Matthews, since we're done with our little...experiment, Father Kirk and I have some business to finish."

Father Kirk closed his eyes, embarrassed for his friend, and for the total lack of manners shown by the Bishop. "I'll walk you out, James." He stood up.

Reverend James stood up. "That's okay, Father Kirk, I know the way. Besides," he nodded to the Bishop, "I've kept you from your *business* long enough." The preacher didn't wait for a response. He turned and strode out the door.

CHAPTER 15

Reverend James looked across the dining room table to where his mother sat. Mary Matthews stared back at him and nodded her head.

"Yes, I'm sure that was embarrassing for you, James."

It was almost six o'clock at night and the sun was low in the sky. The preacher had skulked out of Father Kirk's office the night before and walked the mile to his house. He had tossed and turned the whole night and felt like he hadn't slept at all. After a busy Monday at the office, he couldn't wait to get to his mother's house, where they often dined together on Monday nights, and he had been a few minutes early. His mother was in the middle of trying to digest more than her food.

Her little Cape Cod house was four blocks from their church. There was a small entranceway with a closet just inside the door. The living room was to the left, dining room on the right and the kitchen down the hall with a connecting archway into the dining room. The stairway to the three small bedrooms upstairs was dominated by an aluminum rail and a chair parked at the bottom that glided Mary up and down as needed. She had considered turning the living room into a bedroom and not dealing with the stairs at all, but the only bathtub in the house was upstairs, and Mary loved her baths. She had listened to her son tell the events from yesterday, and she knew a bath would be in order tonight.

"Bishop Walters treated me like a child," the preacher explained, "and Patrick had a hard time even looking at me." He picked at the meatloaf in front of him and considered another bite of the candied sweet potatoes. Ultimately, he chose his favorite; green bean casserole topped with French onions. He took a spoonful and ate it.

Mary watched her son and remembered the many meals they had together since his wife, Thelma, had died. She looked at the empty seat that John Matthews had sat in hundreds, perhaps a thousand times. *No one should have to bury their child,* she thought. Still, the surreal subject matter she was dealing with now was just as overwhelming, if not more so.

She looked down at her plate and still couldn't force her appetite to appear. Mary shoved her plate aside and resigned herself to nuking the food later.

"James, I've never known you to lie to me, but this is impossible to believe. I know the Lord works in mysterious ways, but…my son, a healer?"

"I know, Momma. If I hadn't seen it with my own two eyes, I wouldn't believe it, either."

The preacher's mind was a jumble of confusing thoughts. He had trouble focusing on any one thought as his mind raced and jumped from one fragmented thought to another.

"What if we don't try to prove it, James?"

The preacher was intrigued by the suggestion. "What do you mean, Momma?"

"If, in fact, you did heal that boy—and let's just say you did—and then you couldn't heal Susan, God would have a reason."

Reverend James sat up straight, and his eyes grew wide as the memory dropped into consciousness. "That's it!" He put his fork down on the plate and grabbed the edges of the table with his hands. "Great-Grandfather Carlton—well, the vision I had of him—told me there would be three conditions on my gift—the gift of healing he gave me."

"I can't believe we are even seriously discussing this." Mary slid her chair back and fanned herself with her hands.

"He said I would have to learn those conditions for myself." The preacher was back in the chapel, now, his mind reliving that dream that wasn't a dream. He saw himself floating off the ground; his legless great-grandfather floating as well. He heard the words anew and was revitalized. *Now, how to go about figuring out the conditions?*

"Momma, I don't have any proof. I'm not sure the boy that I healed, Tommy, even knows what happened to him. After I had healed him, he looked frightened and ran away."

"You said he was unconscious after he got hit," Mary offered.

"Yes."

"That was all that happened? He just got up and ran away?"

"Yes, but—I mean—he looked at Luke and me and took off."

Mary thought for a moment. "Luke didn't say anything to him?"

"No, he was choking at the time."

"Why was Luke choking?"

Reverend James hesitated. He had left out the part about nearly strangling Luke to death. Now he had no choice. "When I saw Luke get out of the car, something inside of me just snapped. I didn't want to tell you this, Momma, but I almost strangled him to death." The preacher prepared for the tongue-lashing he knew was coming. He heard laughter.

"Good!" Mary laughed even louder when James' startled look washed across his face. "Lord forgive me, but, good! Somebody needs to straighten that boy out."

Reverend James watched his mother in disbelief. His standard for measuring his faith had always been the example set by his mother, and now, here she was, laughing at his near murder of Luke. Life had just become even more confusing.

Mary saw the look on his face and explained, "James, I'm glad you didn't kill Luke. That would have been very bad." She stopped laughing and grew serious. "There is a part of me that believes Luke would have gotten what he deserved. Only five years for killing Thelma!" A tear rolled down Mary's cheek, and she decided to shut up. She would have to say extra prayers for Luke tonight. She did not hate the man, but the resentment she felt had shown itself. *How could they let him out of jail after only five years?* She bowed her head and prayed to let go of it.

"You really loved her, didn't you, Momma?"

Mary heard the rumbling of his voice, but not the question. "Huh?"

"Thelma," he continued. "You loved Thelma, didn't you?"

Mary nodded and remembered the times she had spent with her son's wife. Mary's husband had died just ten days after John Matthews was born. It was April 15, tax day, 1994. It was a Friday afternoon. Quentin Matthews had battled kidney cancer for over a year. He had fought hard to survive long enough to see his grandson born. Thelma had spent the next two years bringing the baby over to Mary. She told Mary it was because she needed the help, but in truth, it was Mary who was helped. Thelma was special that way. When someone needed help, she was always there. "Yes, James, I loved her very much."

"Well, I'm glad I didn't kill him," the preacher concluded. "He is the only witness I have that this healing worked."

Mary thought about that. "Now, that's a possibility."

Reverend James gave his mom that I-don't-get-it look.

"A witness. Jesus often had a witness to his healings."

"Yes, but Luke wasn't at the Catholic church when I tried to…" Reverend James stopped in mid-sentence as he made the connection.

"You said that there would be conditions on your—your healings." Mary shrugged her shoulders.

"You think that Luke has to be there? When I heal somebody?"

"I don't know, James, but it would give you somewhere to start. To tell the truth, I'm not sure how to feel about all this."

Reverend James glanced at his watch and then at his half-eaten dinner. "Momma, I need to go." He waved his hands toward the food. "Would you mind?"

"No, child, I don't mind. You just be careful."

The preacher pushed his chair back and walked over to his mother. He planted a gentle kiss on her forehead. "I love you, Momma."

"I love you, too, James." Mary followed her son to the door and hugged him goodbye.

After the preacher left, she cleaned off the dining room table and put the leftovers away. Mary thought about the incredible story she had just heard. She wanted to believe that it was true, but another part of her had a deep sense of foreboding. She brooded only a moment and then put her worries where she knew they belonged. She walked into the living room and sat in her favorite rocker. From the end table next to her, she pulled out her Bible and pulled it to her bosom, wrapping both arms around it like cuddling a baby. She rocked back and forth and began to pray

CHAPTER 16

Luke Jones was sprawled on his couch watching a rerun of *America's Funniest Home Videos* on his dinosaur of a television. Though his eyes were on the television; his mind flashed with the memory of his car striking that boy yesterday. He could still see the light that seemed to come from the preacher's hands and melt into the boy and then—Bam! The kid was like nothing ever happened.

Luke laughed at the guy on the screen who hit a curb and went over the handlebars of his bicycle and planted his face in a flowerbed. He sat up, grabbed the two-liter bottle of Diet Coke off the coffee table, tipped it up, and swallowed hard. He shivered as the rum he had mixed in hit his throat. He lay back down again and turned his attention to the television.

The old Sony twenty-seven-inch television had been sitting on a curb when he'd picked it up. Now it sat on an old wood-framed Zenith console that no longer worked. The rest of the living room was sparse. There was the couch, the coffee table, and a fifty-five gallon plastic waste can in one corner that overflowed with booze bottles and beer cans. There was a screened door that led to the outside and another doorway that led to the eat-in kitchen of the run-down duplex. Luke rented the downstairs, but the upstairs was currently for rent and vacant. Luke liked the privacy and hoped that nobody would rent it any time soon.

He sat upright on the couch when he heard the screen door open. To his disgust, he found Reverend

James standing in the doorway of his apartment. Luke fell off the couch and staggered to his feet. He just stood there and blinked.

Reverend James searched for a way to break the ice. "You always leave your door unlocked?"

The pair just stood and stared at each other.

"Luke?"

Luke was lost in a torrent of thoughts. He saw the preacher's wife as his car slammed into the driver's side door. This vision never left him, no matter how much booze he drank. Except for that time two weeks ago when he had robbed the collection basket at the preacher's church, he had not been within two hundred yards of Reverend James until the accident yesterday. Now, a day later, here he was again. *What in the hell is going on?*

"Luke!" The preacher tried again to permeate the shock and alcoholic haze that he surmised Luke was stuck in.

Luke snapped out of his drunken state. "You stay away from me, Preacher. You tried to kill me."

Reverend James walked behind the couch and stopped in front of the kitchen doorway. "Trust me, Luke, I don't *want* to be here, I truly don't." The preacher meant it. He watched Luke turn around to face him and struggled to keep the anger from taking over his mind. He could still feel the joy of his hands around Luke's throat, the sheer power and vengeance of cutting off his air supply. The next feeling had been the guilt for having enjoyed the attack so much. He forced himself to focus on today.

"Luke, I'm here because I need your help."

"I don't want you here. This is my house, MY house, dammit, now go!!!" Luke pointed toward the door in case the preacher had forgotten where it was. Luke got flustered when the preacher didn't move. "Get the hell out of here and just leave me alone."

Reverend James could see he had provoked Luke, and he tried to calm him down a little by backing up. He stopped when he heard the sound of a beer can being crushed under his foot.

"Luke, I can't believe this, either, I can't, but do you remember what happened yesterday when you ran over that boy, Tommy?"

"I don't want to remember yesterday. I wanted to forget yesterday. I want you to leave, and I want to forget you were ever here."

"Luke, you don't understand. I don't understand, but if I'm correct, I need a witness, and it has to be you." The preacher saw the curious look on Luke's face so he continued, "You see, Luke, you were there when I healed that boy, but you weren't there when I tried to heal Susan, and it didn't work. That's why I'm here. I think you have to be there in order for the healing to work."

Luke went from curious to confused in a heartbeat. "What in the hell are you talking about?"

The preacher sighed and willed himself to be patient. "You remember what happened with the boy, right?"

"I remember you tried to kill me. That kid wasn't my fault; I didn't have a stop sign. That kid must've crashed the stop sign."

"I'm sorry about choking you. You were standing there and had just hit the kid with your car, and it brought back memories of—of—I just kind of lost my..."

Luke barked at the preacher. "I paid my debt for that, man. I did five years."

"Five years doesn't even begin to pay for what you took from me, Luke!"

"I paid my debt!" Luke rose to his full height and pointed toward the door. "Now get out!"

The preacher didn't get a chance to respond. The screen door burst open, and Tony and Raymond stormed into the room. Raymond had a baseball bat in his hand. They froze where they stood when they saw the preacher.

Raymond whistled and shook his head in disbelief. He walked over to the preacher with the business end of the bat pointed at him. "You are the last person I expected to see here, Preacher." He raised the bat up to the preacher's head. "You just turn around and keep your mouth shut and you can walk out of here after we leave." He turned the bat toward Luke and his face lit up. "Unfortunately for Luke; he won't be walking anywhere."

Luke made a dash for the door and ran into Tony's fist. The blow knocked him into the wall. Tony twisted Luke's arm behind his back and snatched a handful of hair to lead him back into the room.

"You're pulling my hair? Your sister teach you that?" Luke screamed. He screamed even louder when Tony wrenched his arm further up his back.

"Not smart, Luke," Tony said as he sat Luke down on the end table.

Raymond had been watching Tony handling Luke and was not happy when he turned around and saw the preacher watching as well. With one hand, he swung Reverend James around and shoved him up against the wall. He leaned in close. "Last warning, Reverend James...I don't mind doing my job. As a matter of fact, I kind of like it." Raymond got even closer. "I've never had to hurt a preacher before, but there's a first time for everything." He pulled his mouth away from the preacher's ear and strode over to Tony and Luke, his sardonic laughter echoing off the living room walls.

Raymond grabbed Luke's ankle and swung it up to the table. He took hold of the other ankle and pulled them together and then sat on them. Tony let go of Luke's arm and pulled him flat onto the table by his hair. His other hand reached into his pocket and pulled out the bungee cord he had stuffed there.

Luke reached up and grabbed a handful of Tony's hair and was rewarded for the action with Raymond's big fist to his gut. The blow knocked the wind out of Luke, causing him to let go of Tony. Tony took the opportunity to wrap the bungee cord around the coffee table and Luke's neck. Luke reached for the cord and Raymond smashed the bat into his forearm. Luke tried to sit up but choked when the bungee grew tight around his throat, pulling his head back down to the table.

Tony slapped a pair of handcuffs on Luke's wrists and pulled them over Luke's head. He reached under the table and stretched the bungee cord tautly and wove the bungee hook through the chain of the handcuffs. Now, whenever Luke moved his hands, the bungee cord tightened even more around his neck. It was an effective way to keep Luke's upper body down, yet he could still tilt his head up to see what was about to happen to him. Luke's lower body was going nowhere with Raymond sitting on his ankles.

Tony stood up next to the table and nodded to Raymond, who tossed the bat and watched him catch it. Raymond had a glint in his eye, and his heartbeat quickened. He was jealous that Tony got to do the job, but Jesus had been specific, so that was how it had to be.

Reverend James stood with his forehead up against the wall. He was surprised at the range of emotions flowing through his heart and head. In one way, the thought of Luke getting hurt made him glad, but the next moment he was upset that he felt that way. He sneaked a peek over his shoulder and saw Tony raise the bat up as high as the ceiling would allow.

"Tony, please, man—don't," Luke managed to croak out.

"Too late, Luke. People need to know what happens when you don't pay your debts." Tony gripped the bat hard and brought the fat end down on Luke's knee. A loud crunch followed and Luke shrieked in pain.

Reverend James heard the shriek and jumped toward Tony. He had it in his mind that he was going to take the bat from the larger man. What he was going to do after that hadn't popped into his brain yet. It didn't matter, anyway, since Raymond had anticipated the stupidly noble response and clobbered the preacher in the gut with a curled-up meat hook. The preacher dropped to the ground, looking like a fish out of water. His mouth was opening, but no air was getting in.

"I warned you, Preacher," Raymond barked. "Do that again and I'll use the bat on you next." He nodded to Tony.

Luke was writhing on the table, gurgling sounds emanating from his mouth. Tony hesitated, and then drew a bead on the knee that was still intact. The bat rose to the ceiling once more and crashed down onto the other knee with a resounding crunch. Luke wailed and screamed; his mouth foamed and snot came out his nose and landed on his chin.

Raymond jumped to his feet when he saw the mucus blow out of Luke's nose. "That's disgusting, man!"

Tony wasted no time. He handed the bat to Raymond and unlocked the handcuffs from the howling Luke. He undid the bungee cord and pulled it from around Luke's neck, stuffing the items back into his pockets and heading for the door. He stopped at the door and waited for his partner.

The Healing of Reverend James

Raymond leaned over Reverend James and brought his face in close to the gasping man. "Talk about this to anyone and..." Raymond brought the bat up to the preacher's face and let it bump his nose. "Don't make me hurt you any more." Raymond stood tall and sucked in a deep breath. *God, I love my job,* he thought. He noticed Tony by the door and joined him. The two men left without looking back.

In shock, Luke had tears running down his face. He whimpered and tried not to move. Every little movement caused another bolt of pain to shoot through his legs. Luke lifted his hands up to his neck, his fingers checking to make sure the bungee cord was gone. He shook his head, trying to think through the pain. Then he laughed—a shrill, choking laugh that one might expect to hear in an insane asylum.

The preacher was breathing now, though it took a lot of effort. He rolled onto his belly and worked his way up to his knees. Reverend James heard the cackling. "Why are you laughing?"

Luke moved to look at the preacher and squealed as the pain shot through his legs, "Ouch, shit! Damn that hurts." Luke choked again but was careful to remain still. "That's the second time in two days that I was almost strangled to death!" He laughed and choked and coughed even harder. That quickly morphed into whimpering when he forgot and moved his legs again.

Reverend James didn't even try to figure out how someone in Luke's condition could joke about something like that. He worked his way over to Luke, knelt beside him, and looked him in the eyes. "I need your assistance, Luke. We could help a lot of people."

"If anyone needs help around here, it's me." Luke glared at the preacher, the pain reflected in his eyes.

Reverend James forced his body to straighten, and he pulled both his hands above Luke's chest. "I think I can do something about that." He brought his hands together and started to drop them down on Luke.

Luke slapped the preacher's hands away. "I don't want no witchcraft being performed on me, Reverend James." Luke tried to be defiant, but the pain in his head and his knees was too great. He couldn't block the preacher's hands a second time.

Reverend James dropped his hands onto Luke's chest. The light appeared, radiating out from the preacher's hands and enveloping Luke from head to toe. Luke cried out when he saw the light absorb into his body, and just a second later, watched in disbelief as the light exploded in all directions. The room flashed bright white, and then the light was gone.

The preacher sat back on his haunches and inhaled deeply. Luke sat up on the coffee table and swung his legs over the side, so he was facing Reverend James. His eyes were wide, and his fingers wandered over his kneecaps. They were fine. He looked into the preacher's eyes.

"Now, will you help me?"

CHAPTER 17

Susan Erikson rolled her wheelchair into Father Kirk's study. She stopped immediately when she saw Luke Jones standing near one of the two leather chairs that sat in front of the priest's desk. "Okay, you guys." Susan looked at the two holy men. "This thing is getting a little weird." She glanced at Luke again and tried to hide her discomfort. She waited for a moment, but no response came. "Hey! Can one of you guys fill in the blanks, please?"

Reverend James responded. "When we tried to do this before, you said if I was able to figure out what went wrong that I should let you know." Reverend James nodded toward Luke. "I think that one of the conditions for the healing is that Luke has to be present." He wasn't sure what to say after that comment, so he didn't say anything.

Susan looked at Luke again and back to the preacher. "Okay, Reverend James, it's your gig, but this God of yours has a really twisted sense of humor." Susan couldn't believe these men were here, in the same room. She tried to hide the disdain she felt, but there had been too many conversations with Father Kirk about Luke Jones, and few to none had been kind. "Where do you want me?"

"Right there is fine, Susan. I just want to thank you for agreeing to try this again." The preacher struggled for the right words to say, but none came. "I'm sorry, Susan, I don't know what else to say."

"You don't have to say anything, Reverend," Susan replied.

Father Kirk jumped into the conversation. "Especially, don't say anything to Bishop Walters."

Reverend James looked from face to face, so everyone understood the gravity of the situation. "Whatever happens in this room...stays amongst us." The others nodded when he looked at each them in turn.

Luke had watched the interactions among the three others in the room and had begun to feel like the odd man out. He saw the look on Susan's face when she'd seen him standing in the room and recognized it: loathing. She didn't even try to hide it. *What in the hell am I doing here?*

"Luke." The preacher called his name out again.

"Huh?" Luke answered.

"Please stand over here on the other side of Susan." Reverend James pointed to the other side of the wheelchair, just in case Luke was as lost as the look on his face indicated.

Luke walked next to Susan and pretended he couldn't feel the seething.

Father Kirk walked around his desk and looked at the trio with a mixture of excitement and anxiety. He wondered if Bishop Walters would excommunicate him if he knew they had tried this again. The Bishop had been clear in his communication that the Catholic Church did not wish to support such *activities.* If it had been anybody other than Reverend James, this wouldn't have happened. Having Luke Jones in his office made it all the more difficult.

Patrick wasn't sure if he wanted the healing to work or not; he was sure that he wanted it over. The Bishop would be heading home from his visits to the other churches in the region, and, although unlikely, it was possible he would check in on his way back to Buffalo. The priest shuddered at the thought.

Reverend James kneeled next to Susan. "You ready?"

Susan nodded but failed to keep the apprehension off her face.

"Here we go." Reverend James put his hands together and silently prayed. Then he placed his hands, palms down, on Susan's legs.

Nothing.

All four of the people in the room deflated. The men backed away from Susan, and all started talking at once.

Father Kirk was the loudest. "Okay, we tried. Let's break this up in case the Bishop decides to stop by on his way through."

Reverend James rose and talked to Patrick. "This thing works, Patrick, I swear it does. I just have to figure out what's going wrong."

Luke was stunned that the healing didn't work. He saw the disappointed look on Susan's face and tried to help. "This thing really works, Susan. He just healed me last night." Luke turned to the two men when Susan's response was to grit her teeth and ram the control forward, steering the wheelchair toward the door.

"I'm nervous, James," the priest said, "I just want us all to talk about this later and not in front of Susan."

"Would all of you please just stop!" Susan had swung her wheelchair around and faced the three men, fighting to keep the tears from streaming down her cheeks.

Startled by Susan's outburst, the men stopped talking.

She continued. "I've had three surgeries in the last two years to try to repair the damage to my back. I don't have the money for these new, experimental implants they're doing now, and my insurance refused to pay for them, anyway. I've prayed and prayed, and when I was done with that, I prayed some more." Susan fought for control of her trembling hands. Her voice cracked.

"I knew this wasn't a good idea," Father Kirk said. "I'm sorry, Susan. This is my fault. I should never have agreed to put you through this again."

"I'm sorry, too, Susan," the preacher added, "I was just trying to help. This is all very confusing."

"No, you don't understand." Susan shook her head and tried slow the emotion that desperately wanted to take control of her.

"We're done here," the priest said.

"I don't want to be done," Susan said. "You don't understand what I mean."

"I sure as hell don't understand what's happening." Luke chimed in.

Reverend James and Father Kirk both yelled at Luke to keep quiet, and the three men began bickering with each other. They were so busy pointing fingers at each other that they seemed to forget that Susan was sitting in front of them.

Susan watched the fracas, and her frustration with the situation overwhelmed her. Her emotions took over, and the tears poured from her eyes. She screamed at the men.

"My husband is having an affair and he's going to divorce me!" She covered her face with her hands and wept.

Father Kirk heard the outburst and rushed to her side, cradling his arm around her shoulder and pulling her up against his chest. He glanced at the others and was not surprised to see the stunned look on their faces. He was stunned, himself. He turned his attention back to Susan. "I'm sorry, I didn't know, Susan. Why didn't you tell me?"

Susan looked the priest. There was no malice in her face, just grief. "He doesn't know that I know," she wiped away her tears and more took their place. Reverend James reached over to Father Kirk's desk and snatched a couple of Kleenex tissues from the box. He handed them to the priest.

Father Kirk placed the tissues in Susan's hand. "I'll have a talk with Carl. I can counsel you both."

Susan dabbed at her eyes and shook her head. "No, Father. I appreciate that, but it's too late for that."

"What do you mean?"

"When I first found out, I thought, 'Good, he'll get what he needs, and he will come home to me.' I mean, I can't give him that, anymore." Susan choked back the tears. "First he was late for dinner, then he was late for bed—my bed, anyway. Does he really think I believe he works until ten o'clock at night two to three times a week?"

Father Kirk couldn't keep quiet. "Susan, please, I know Carl, let me talk to him?"

"You know Carl?" Susan asked. "I thought I knew Carl, Father, but the truth is, until something like this happens, you really don't know who someone is." Susan glanced at Luke and Reverend James. The empathy she found in the preacher's eyes helped. She turned back to Father Kirk. "No, Father, I don't want you to talk to my husband. Either he will stay with me for who I am, the way that I am, or I want him to leave." Susan took a deep breath and clenched her jaw, "In sickness and health, right?"

Father Kirk was speechless. There are times when words fail even a priest.

"I'm sorry, Father, all I have left is hope." She backed her wheelchair up and left the priest kneeling. Susan glanced at Reverend James and Luke. "After all, you've got to believe in miracles for one to happen, right?"

Susan turned her wheelchair around and rolled toward the door. Father Kirk rose to his feet, and Susan stopped in the doorway, talking over her shoulder. "Reverend James?"

"Yes, Susan?"

"If you figure out what's going wrong, you call me." She didn't wait for an answer, and rolled down the hall and out of sight.

CHAPTER 18

Reverend James sat across the table from Maya Richards at the local Applebee's in Lakewood, just three miles northwest of Jamestown. Maya had listened to the events of the past two days without comment. That had allowed the preacher to work through the details uninterrupted and had given Maya a chance to collect her thoughts. It wasn't the kind of conversation she had hoped for on their first date, but they were here, together. She was happy they weren't at the church office going over the same old day-to-day details.

Maya had known something was wrong when Reverend James had walked into his office this morning. He had seemed preoccupied, and for a brief moment she considered that he was having second thoughts about their date. Ten minutes later he had called her to join him in the office, and the jumbled mess of details came pouring out of him. They were interrupted by a phone call before he could finish, and he had to leave. The next time she saw him, he was sitting in his Jeep Liberty in her driveway just down from the church. He was right on time and had surprised her with a single white rose.

He said the white rose had always symbolized a new beginning for him. Thelma and he had welcomed every new leader of any denomination into the area with a white rose, for many years. It touched her deeply that he would choose this for her on their first date. The connection to Thelma didn't bother her one bit. If anything, she was even more delighted to receive it because of that connection. At forty-nine years old, Maya knew better than to be jealous of the cherished memory of his departed wife and her longtime friend.

Maya was very concerned about one issue in particular. She waited until she saw Reverend James swallow his food.

"I don't like you being involved with that Jesus Juarez and his thugs." Maya got a bad feeling just talking about them. "That bunch is bad news."

"I know. I'm sorry we even have to discuss this on our first date, Maya." The preacher could still feel the pain from Raymond's fist radiating from his belly. "I just—I didn't expect any of this."

Maya decided to be blunt. "I'm not happy about any of this healing business. It just doesn't seem real, but I'm willing to listen."

Reverend James was surprised by the comment and incapable of a quick response.

"I just wanted you to know you can talk to me about anything, Reverend James: John, Thelma, this healing business, whatever." Maya had never tiptoed around sensitive subjects and wasn't about to start now.

"On one condition."

"One condition?" she asked.

"Yes. Please drop the 'Reverend;' it's James, just James."

Maya liked that, and it showed on her face. Maya had waited when they shared the appetizer sampler platter, looking for the right time. She had known Reverend James for twenty-nine years and yet, at this moment, she felt as awkward as a twelve-year-old girl. But she wasn't twelve anymore. She stretched her hand across the grains of the wooden tabletop and brushed against his.

He was surprised by his own reaction. He had forced himself to forget the feeling of a woman's hand on his, at least in a romantic context. When she brushed his hand, the feelings rushed back and the moment was at once both comforting and intimidating. He wanted to reach out and take her hand in his, but he was nervous and confused.

"Are you done with your appetizer?" the waitress asked. "Can I take your plate?"

The preacher nodded, and Maya pulled her hand away when he sat back in the booth.

"Your dinner will be out shortly," the waitress added. She retrieved the appetizer plate and left.

Maya wanted to finish the conversation before dinner arrived. "Have you decided what you're going to do about all this business with Luke?"

"We're going to meet in the chapel tomorrow afternoon," he answered. "We were standing outside of Patrick's church after we failed to heal—attempted to heal—Susan, and I—I needed some time to think. Also, I needed time to pick up your rose before our date."

Maya grinned. "The rose was perfect, Rev—I mean, the rose was perfect, James." Maya liked the sound his name made rolling off her lips. "Are you sure he'll be there? Luke, I mean."

"He'll be there." He smiled knowingly.

"What are you hiding?"

"I told him I'd give him ten bucks for showing up."

"James!"

"I know this works, Maya." His demeanor became serious. "I don't know what all three of the conditions are, or even why there are conditions, but I know this works and I know I need Luke Jones." He paused as the gravity of what he'd just said resounded through his brain. He looked into Maya's eyes. "I haven't even had time to think about that. I never imagined in my wildest dreams that I would make a statement like that." He remembered the powerful, wonderful feelings of his hands squeezing Luke's throat; and the absolute horror of what he had almost done. *Just think,* he pondered, *if I had killed Luke, there would never have been a healing.*

That thought was still ricocheting around his brain when Maya's voice filtered through his thoughts. "James, are you still with me?"

"I'm sorry, Maya. I guess the reality of all this...this...unreal stuff is starting to sink in."

"Yes, I suppose it is. One minute you were here and the next minute you were gone." She smiled to let him know it was not a problem. She had noticed the dark circles under his eyes and the drooping eyelids. "I have an idea." She floated the comment like it was a thought that had just occurred to her.

"What's that?"

"You look tired, James."

He nodded.

"How about getting them to box our dinner up, and you can take me home?"

The preacher was stunned. "But—our date?"

"I didn't say our date was over."

The waitress returned to the table and placed the spicy Asian riblet platter in front of Reverend James and the three-cheese and chicken penne platter in front of Maya.

Maya asked the waitress for two to-go boxes and the check. She turned back to the preacher. "We aren't going to get many more warm nights like this, James. Let's go to my house and eat our dinner on the porch swing. I can put out TV trays, and we can enjoy the breeze and watch the first leaves falling off the trees."

Reverend James looked down at his plate of riblets. They looked good, but he wasn't hungry anyway; mostly, he was tired. The stress of the past three weeks, losing John, and all the other details to do with the healings were catching up to him. He could almost feel the cool autumn breeze across his face.

"Dinner on your porch sounds wonderful, Maya."

On cue, the waitress showed up with the to-go boxes and the check.

Reverend James dropped his debit card onto the bill, and they transferred the food from their plates into the Styrofoam containers. When the waitress returned with the check, Maya insisted on leaving the tip. She was thrilled when they got up to leave that Reverend

James reached out and took her hand to help her out of the booth.

***

Maya had set the TV trays up as promised, although they didn't eat much of the food. They had talked for what had seemed minutes, but was actually hours. Maya sat through his rehashing of the events the night he had broken the cross and everything that had happened since. She listened to him talk about his loneliness since Thelma died and how he had filled up his time with church activities and John's basketball life. He fell apart when Maya had told him how much she missed Thelma as well.

When he had cried, she had pulled him down and put his head in her lap and just kept rocking the swing. Back and forth and back and forth; her hands stroked his hair and neck in time to the tempo of the sway. He didn't remember falling asleep. He woke up almost two hours later, still in her lap, the tender touch of her fingers still on him. He chastised her gently for allowing him to make her sit so long in the chill of the autumn night. She just smiled and said he had kept her warm.

The most memorable part was their good-night kiss, the softness of his lips; a gentle, lingering kiss, which sent waves of pleasure down her spine.

On the way home, Reverend James had felt guilty for enjoying the kiss so much. Then he remembered the conversation he had had with Thelma just days after John's birth, when his father had died from cancer.

Thelma had told him that if anything ever happened to her, she wanted him to move on with his life and not waste it pining for a past love. He argued that his love for her would always exist and could never die, even if she did. She had smiled and told him that she felt the same, but wasn't going to spend her life being lonely, should he die. Thelma was beautiful and wise. Even now, her words helped to bring peace to his life.

CHAPTER 19

Reverend James sat in the second row of his chapel trying to pray. Luke Jones was pacing up and down the center aisle of the little chapel. He was irritated that Reverend James decided to keep the ten dollars he'd been promised for showing up until they were finished. He forced his mind to focus on the fact the preacher had healed his legs; at least he tried.

"Do you have to keep walking back and forth like that?" Reverend James growled. He had always come to the chapel to clear his mind, but never had to deal with anyone pacing before. The fact that it was Luke Jones doing the pacing didn't help.

"That crap at the Catholic church was embarrassing." Luke continued to pace. "I don't know what could've gone wrong. I mean…" Luke stopped in front of the pew where Reverend James was sitting and stared at the preacher. "Are you going to figure this thing out or not?"

Reverend James stiffened. "That's what I'm trying to do."

"You're just sitting there staring at that cross like you're waiting for it to talk to you or something."

"I'm trying to pray; only someone keeps walking up and down the aisle." Reverend James didn't like looking up at Luke, so he rose and faced him. "You should try praying some time, Luke. Lord knows your soul could use it."

"At least I'm not a church preacher that broke my grandfather's cross and am running around like a

153

crazy man telling everybody I can heal people when I can't."

"First, it's my great-grandfather's cross, and second of all, the healing works and you know it!"

"Maybe we should break that cross again. Maybe you could smack your head on that table again." Luke was proud of his ability to come up with the idea himself.

The preacher scowled. "The vision I saw said there would be three conditions on the gift of healing and those I must figure out for myself." He glared at Luke. "The only one I know of, to this point, is that *you* have to be there."

Luke couldn't handle the stare and started pacing again.

Reverend James decided not to bother him about the pacing anymore; it was better than listening to the man talk. The preacher sat back down. Leaning forward, he placed his elbows on his knees and his face in his hands, lost in thought. Once again, he was jarred out of the quiet moment by Luke in his face.

"Did you even hear me?" Luke was hunched over, and his breath was awful.

Spurred on by the halitosis and the nearness of Luke, Reverend James stood up and pushed Luke backward. "Get out of my face, Luke, and get some mints or gum.

"I could do that if you would give me the money you promised me for showing up here today," Luke whined.

The Healing of Reverend James

"I told you I would give you the money when we are finished." The preacher stepped up onto the altar, since the room felt much smaller with Luke in it. There was nowhere to run.

"Well, if you would try talking to me instead of praying and meditating all the time, maybe we could figure this thing out."

Reverend James shot back, "Praying clears my mind, Luke; it has since I was a child. I'll say it again; you should try it some time."

"Yeah, well, praying isn't talking. I know I'm not your favorite person on this planet. Trust me, I know that. But you don't have anyone else to talk to about this. From what you told me, you and I are the only ones that have seen this thing work."

"What did you say?" The preacher stood wide-eyed in front of Luke.

Luke hesitated. "I said praying isn't talking."

"No, after that."

Luke was lost. He thought for a moment. "I'm not your favorite person on the planet?"

Reverend James inhaled; his excitement filled the small chapel. "You said we were the only ones that had seen this work."

"Yeah?"

The preacher bolted for the chapel door and opened it. He turned to Luke. "Whatever you do, don't leave. The preacher disappeared through the door.

Luke rushed to the door and yelled after the preacher. "Where are you going? What about my money?"

The preacher's voice echoed through the church to Luke. "I'll give you twenty when I get back."

Luke liked the sound of that; he'd just doubled his money. He walked over to the pew and sat down.

CHAPTER 20

Luke had fallen asleep, but woke up when he heard the chapel door open. He had been leaning up against the wall and pushed himself upright trying to get the kink out of his neck. When he turned around, he saw Susan Erikson roll through the chapel door that Reverend James was holding open. Luke rose from the pew and stepped into the aisle.

Susan looked nervous. She looked around the room, and her eyes came to rest on the cross. "That's the cross you told me about, right?"

"That's right, Susan." Reverend James came up beside Susan and kneeled on the floor. "That was carved by my great-grandfather in 1885 in Deland, Florida." He turned and looked into her eyes. "Rumor has it he carved it with his bare hands and the fire of his faith."

Susan wasn't even going to try to imagine that one.

"What the hell is going on?" Luke asked.

Reverend James wasn't going to let Luke's bad manners ruin his mood. "Lighten up, Luke. You're the one that figured this out."

Susan gave Luke two thumbs up.

Luke was still confused. "Well, if I figured it out, how come I don't know what it is?"

The preacher decided it was time to enlighten Luke. "You said that we were the only people that had seen the healing work, and that's when it hit me."

Nobody moved.

"It's a condition of the gift," he continued, "We are the only people that *can* be present when we heal somebody! You, me, and the person we are healing."

"I don't understand."

"Luke, when I healed the boy you hit, it was only you, me, and him. When I healed you, it was only you and me." The preacher paused to let the information sink in. "The two times I tried to heal Susan, there were other people around, so it didn't work."

Luke was silent, and then his face lit up as the lightbulb turned on. "You mean we're the only two *allowed* to be present when you're healing someone?"

"Yes, I think that is the case. I believe that is another condition of the healing." The preacher smiled at the thought and nodded to Susan. "I know a way we can find out for sure. Susan, would you like to find out if our theory is correct?"

Susan's lip was trembling. "I'm here. Let's do it!"

"Well, then, what are we waiting for? Let's be getting on with the layin' on of hands, man," Luke blurted out.

"Luke, just come over here and hold Susan's hand or kneel next to her, please." Reverend James waited until Luke kneeled beside Susan and offered her his hand. She hesitated and then gripped his hand tight and nodded to the preacher.

Reverend James knew this was the moment of truth. Beads of sweat formed on his forehead and the anticipation in the room was palpable. He placed his hands together and mouthed a silent prayer. Susan and Luke watched, wide-eyed as his hands descended onto Susan's thigh.

A brilliant flash of light shot out of the preacher's hands and covered Susan from head to toe. The light seemed to soak into Susan's body. There was a final flash of light, and it was gone.

Susan and Luke started screaming at the same time.

"Susan!" the preacher yelled, panic in his voice. "What's the matter? Are you all right?"

Luke hollered at the same time. "Let go of my hand! You're crushing it!"

Susan released her grip and burst into tears, the sobs racking her body. Luke and Reverend James stared at each other.

"Is she okay?" Luke asked.

The preacher's mind raced with thoughts of 911 and an ambulance hauling Susan away. He was in the middle of being questioned by the police when Susan spoke, bringing him back to reality.

"I feel…" She broke down in tears again, and both men were silent, waiting for Susan to speak. "I feel your hands on my thigh!" Susan choked. The preacher felt her thigh muscles move. "I can wiggle my toes!"

Susan fell into Reverend James' arms and wept tears of joy. She held him tight and allowed the tears to rain down her cheeks.

For once in his life, Luke was quiet and just watched. The two men allowed Susan to let out the powerful emotion until her tears began to slow.

She finally pulled away from the preacher and turned to Luke.

"I'm sorry about your hand, Luke. I guess I wasn't expecting—I didn't know that this would really work."

Luke held his hand up and moved it around for her to see. "Nothing broken, no problem."

"Susan," the preacher interrupted, "do you think you could stand?"

Susan wiped away the tears from her cheek and looked at the blanket covering her legs. "I don't know, my legs are atrophied from not using them—at least, they were." Susan put her hands on her thighs and shook her head in disbelief when she felt them on her legs. She started crying again.

Reverend James remained patient. He could only imagine the thoughts and emotions that were exploding through Susan. "You take all the time you need. When you're ready, and if you want to, Luke and I will help you up."

Susan nodded. "I want to try." She took a deep breath and dried her tears again. "I want to try right now."

The preacher rose and offered his hand. Luke did the same. Before grabbing their hands, Susan reached down and released the safety strap that held her in the wheelchair. She pulled the blanket off her legs and was surprised to see the fullness underneath her clothing. Out of habit, she bent over and moved the leg rests out of the way. Then she reached out and took Reverend James' hand and reached out her other hand to Luke. The two men braced themselves as Susan pulled herself to a standing position in one quick motion. She began to fall forward and was shocked when her right leg moved. Her foot landed a little forward, and she balanced, the muscles in her lower body responding like a normal person's.

"Oh, dear Lord," she looked at Luke and then glanced at the preacher, "I'm standing! I can feel my muscles working!"

Reverend James had felt her body tremble. "Do you think you could walk?"

Susan appeared startled by the suggestion at first, but she set her jaw and responded. "I think I can." She surprised the men and released their hands.

"I know I can!"

She stood for a moment, gathered herself, and took a step forward, then another. She was in front of the altar now and surprised the men again when she stepped up the four inches onto the altar and turned back toward them.

Joy filled her face, and she cautiously stepped back down and took the two steps back to where she had started. "I can walk!" Susan burst into tears and threw her arms around the preacher again.

"Thank you, Reverend James, thank you so much." She clung to him until she remembered Luke, "Thank you, too, Luke."

Luke was happy she remembered he was there, but wasn't sure what to say. "You're welcome," was all the he managed to get out. His mind was reeling with what had happened and was busy with other thoughts. Those thoughts were interrupted again when Susan shrieked.

"My husband!" The thought rampaged through her brain. "I've got to tell my husband."

She took a step back and searched the preacher's eyes. She hadn't considered all the details when she'd agreed to the healing.

"*What* do I tell my husband?"

"Tell him the truth," Reverend James said. He tried not to show the pain his poor eardrum had suffered when Susan had shrieked.

Susan reached down to her wheelchair and lifted her backpack that was wrapped around the handles. Another item she hadn't thought about popped into her brain. "What do I do with the wheelchair?"

Reverend James hadn't considered that issue, either. "For now, take it with you; just in case."

Susan was startled by the comment. "Just in case? You mean you're not sure if this is permanent?"

"Of course it's permanent," Luke chimed in. "Reverend James just wants to be sure you have it in case your legs get tired. Right, Reverend?"

Reverend James was sure of one thing: he didn't like Luke Jones answering for him. But, when he thought about it, he agreed with him. "Luke's right, Susan. Keep it until you're sure you don't need it—then donate it to someone who does."

"There won't *be* anyone who needs a wheelchair with you around!"

Susan's cheery words rang in the preacher's ears, but for some reason, he felt very tired. "I'll walk you to your car, Susan."

"I like the sound of that," Susan replied. She tossed the book bag into the seat of the wheelchair and pushed it out the chapel door when the preacher opened it.

"Reverend, we gonna meet tomorrow—to talk about all this?" Luke asked.

"That's a good idea, Luke. How about ten o'clock, right back here in the chapel?"

"Oh, yeah, sure—I'll be here," Luke said. "Aren't you forgetting something?" Luke rubbed his two fingers together. He wanted his money.

The preacher held up five fingers and mouthed the words "five minutes." Then he escorted Susan out the door.

Luke watched the chapel door close. He walked over and looked through the window. Once he was sure the preacher was in the parking lot, he turned back into the little chapel and rubbed his hands together with dollar signs dancing in his head. "I'm rich!" He shouted to the empty room. "I'm going to be filthy rich!"

CHAPTER 21

"Everything I told you was absolutely true, Jennifer. I'm gonna be rich!"

Luke had told Jennifer the whole story. The problem was it wasn't the first time Jennifer had heard a story about how rich Luke was going to be. They were standing on Jennifer's porch, and she had made sure she blocked the entrance to the house.

"Keep your voice down. Your daughter is taking a nap." Jennifer had her hands on her hips. "Are you drunk again?" She sniffed the air. "I don't smell any booze."

"Sober as a judge. I'm telling you the truth, Jennifer. You've got to believe me!"

"That's where your wrong, Luke. I don't have to believe you." It had been a long time since Luke had been standing in front of her sober. Jennifer decided it was time for a long overdue conversation.

"I don't believe Reverend James healed your knees. I don't believe you're his personal witness. I don't believe you're ever gonna stay sober, and I don't believe you ever intended to put a ring on my finger."

Luke was stunned. "You still want one?"

Jennifer remembered the funny, lovable young man who had swept her off her feet. Luke had had a job at the Cummins diesel plant right after graduation. He was making good money and had a great car, and she had looked forward to their life together. He had taken care of himself back then. He loved music like she did. They used to drive to Beach 10 at the Peninsula in Erie,

Pennsylvania on their days off. Those days on the beach were the most carefree of her life. Then she got pregnant.

At first, after the shock wore off, it had seemed like it was going to be okay. They'd gotten an apartment together, and Luke had gone through the motions of wanting to be a father. Then he'd started showing up late after "just one beer." The guys wanted to go out, and why shouldn't he be allowed to go out; he worked hard enough; he deserved it. When he hadn't shown up at the hospital for the birth of Jasmine, she was furious. It had gone downhill from there, and she'd wanted to end it when he'd gotten drunk on that Sunday morning and killed Reverend James' wife, Thelma.

She should have walked away then, but Jasmine had been just old enough to know Daddy was going away for a long time, and she'd begged her not to say she would never see him again. Luke had sworn he was reborn. He'd promised to be a model prisoner and come back and marry her and stay sober. She'd seen him every two weeks, making the drive to the Elmira prison, over thirty miles each way. When he'd gotten out, he'd been in great shape. He'd had a lot of time to work out, he'd said. He'd even landed a job through one of his old high school friends, and for a while it had seemed everything was going to be fine. He'd even been putting money away for a ring. Then she'd found out she was pregnant again. Luke had gotten drunk the next day. The dream had become a nightmare, and that nightmare was staring her in the face.

She was tired of waiting for him to grow up. This was the nightmare's last shot.

"If I can have the man I fell in love with, the man that made me laugh…a man that will love and take care of his daughters and me, then the answer is yes. Until then, I want you to leave."

"You want me to leave? Fine, I'll leave." Luke stormed down the stairs and strode to his Caprice. He opened the door to the familiar groan. "You just wait 'til you see my picture in the paper. Then you'll wish you had believed me."

Luke plopped down in the car and started it up. Dirt flew everywhere as he used the gas pedal to emphasize his point, careening backward out of the driveway. He rammed it into drive and tore off down the street.

Jennifer watched her would-be husband drive away. She managed to keep it together as she opened up the screen door, but she stumbled into the empty living room and dropped onto her couch. Softly, she began to cry.

CHAPTER 22

Reverend James opened the side door of his church, about three minutes late for his ten o'clock meeting with Luke. He was surprised to see Susan Erikson seated in the front pew. Next to Susan was a middle-aged Latina woman the preacher did not know. He recognized the long aluminum stick with the red rings around the base that she held, as that used by a blind person. Reverend James walked over to the women.

"Hi, Susan. You look well this morning. I hope everything went well last night?"

"My husband was so excited—well after he got over the initial shock. We cried and prayed together most of the night."

The preacher took note of the weary eyes. "That's wonderful! He handled it pretty well, then?" Reverend James had wondered how her husband would cope with his wife *walking* through their door.

"Yes, he did pretty well." Susan hesitated and said, "He wouldn't believe the part about the healing, however. He believes it was the power of prayer…sorry."

"No need to be sorry. He could be right." The preacher had considered the possibility of denial. He had seen too many people in his life make up facts to explain the unexplainable. It seemed to be human nature. He turned his attention to Susan's friend.

"I haven't had the pleasure of meeting your friend."

167

The woman lifted her chin and extended her hand. A smile spread across her face. "Hi, Reverend James, I'm Anita Tomasina."

The preacher shook her hand. "Hello, Anita. Susan told you I could help you see again?"

"Well, I've been blind since birth, but Susan told me what you did for her, and I...Well, I'm a little bit nervous, to tell the truth."

He looked around the pews and back to Anita. "Well, as soon as Luke gets here, and God willing, of course, we can try. It doesn't hurt." He looked to Susan for confirmation. "Right, Susan?"

Susan nodded and then said it out loud for the benefit of Anita. "No, it didn't hurt me, but Reverend James, Luke is already here." She pointed to the chapel door. "He's in the chapel."

Reverend James was surprised and turned to look at the chapel door.

Susan continued, "I told him about Anne when he called me last night."

"He called you last night?"

"Yes," Susan replied, "I wasn't going to answer the phone because my husband and I were...dealing with all this, but he called my home line. We still keep an answering machine on that line, and when I heard Luke's voice, I picked it up." Susan took a breath. "He said to be here at ten. Well, here we are."

The menagerie of thoughts rolling through the preacher's head caused his eyes to flutter. "What did your husband say?"

The Healing of Reverend James

"He was in the other room, thank God!" Susan was grateful her husband hadn't heard Luke on the answering machine. He'd had enough to deal with at that time. "I didn't tell him because—because—well, because of the history between you two." Susan cringed and hoped she hadn't said too much.

"I understand," was all the preacher could manage. "Would you please excuse me for a minute?" Reverend James didn't wait for an answer and headed for the chapel door.

***

Reverend James charged into the chapel to find Luke standing by the second pew. He stopped with Luke's cheery greeting.

"Good morning, Reverend James. How you doin'?"

"Why did you call Susan and ask her to bring someone here?" The preacher wasn't in the mood for Luke's pleasantries.

"You want to help people, don't you?"

Reverend James wasn't sure what was wrong. Something didn't feel right. Luke standing there with that innocent look plastered on his face rubbed him the wrong way.

"I didn't tell you to call Susan."

"Well, excuse me, Reverend James, but what were you gonna do? Walk down the street, stopping every cripple you see, saying—hello, crippled person, how would you like to be healed today?"

Reverend James hadn't thought of that. He hadn't thought of anything after the healing yesterday. He'd struggled to get through the day and gone to bed early. It was almost comforting to have Luke return to his snide, demeaning nature. "No, no—of course not."

"Well, what then?" Luke challenged.

"I don't know," replied the preacher. "I guess I thought we'd talk about it first."

"All I did was ask Susan if she knew anybody that needed our help. What is so bad about that?" Luke smiled and gestured toward the chapel door. "Smile a little bit, Reverend James. Relax, we have work to do."

The preacher was tired. He glared at Luke and fought the nagging feeling he had that something was wrong. After all, he was anxious to help Anita, glad that his newfound gift would be tested again. *If it works today, then we've got it all figured out,* the preacher thought. *Well, at least the first two conditions.* Luke had a point; they would have to figure out a way to make people aware that he could help them.

Reverend James shook the thought out of his head. Was Luke right again? *Did I really just think that?* He chuckled out loud at the irony.

What's so funny? Luke asked.

"I just thought that you were right," replied the preacher, "we have work to do."

CHAPTER 23

Reverend James was on his knees and faced Anita, who was sitting in the back pew of the chapel. "I'm sorry Susan can't be with you, Anita. It doesn't work like that."

Anita fidgeted in the pew and tried to remain calm. "I understand, Reverend. Susan told me what she went through before it worked for her."

Reverend James thought about Father Kirk. *Did he know about Susan, yet?* Normally, Susan would be working in the office at the Catholic church right now, so, he must know something. The preacher made a mental note to see Patrick soon—today even. He turned his attention back to Susan.

"Well, hopefully we won't have to put you through all that. Luke, would you join us, please?"

Luke looked a little startled and took a couple of steps closer to Anita and the preacher. "I'm here. Let's do this." He fought to keep his focus on Anita.

"Are you okay?" The preacher asked. Luke seemed a little uncomfortable.

"Yeah. Yes, I'm fine."

Reverend James lingered on Luke and finally decided it was time. He brought his hands up to his chest as if in prayer.

"Okay, Anita, here we go." He wished he had chosen different words, but shrugged it off.

Anita tensed with apprehension now that the moment was here. Reverend James gently touched her thigh with his hands.

Nothing.

The preacher immediately glared at Luke. Luke tried not to do it, but he glanced over his shoulder toward the altar. Reverend James followed Luke's gaze and looked right into a camera lens.

Click.

Reverend James was astonished. Lying on the floor, hiding behind the first pew, with a camera in his hand, was a small weasel-faced white man. Reverend James was furious with Luke. Of course it was Luke. Now he knew why his suspicions had been raised earlier.

"Is everything alright?" Anita sensed the tension in the room.

"It will be in a minute, Anita. I have a problem I have to take care of." The preacher bore into the man's eyes, and his finger pointed to the chapel door. The weasel-faced man rose to his feet and quickly snapped off a couple more pictures.

"Out!" was the only word the preacher could manage. He was afraid he would explode with rage if he spoke any more.

"My name is David Broombau," the man offered, "and I was invited here..." The man glared at Luke. "...obviously for no purpose."

Luke opened his mouth to speak, but was interrupted by the preacher.

"Don't you say a word, Luke." Reverend James turned and opened the door of the chapel.

David was going to give the preacher a piece of his mind, but the look on Reverend James' face made him change his mind. He charged out the door and deftly spun around, brought the camera up, and snapped some rapid-fire photos. The door slammed in his face.

***

Susan was startled by the appearance of the little man bursting from the chapel door and the fact that he was taking pictures. The door slammed and for one terrifying moment, she was certain he was going to take her picture. In a panic, she covered her face with her hands. A moment later she peeked through her fingers and was relieved to see that the man had walked out of the side door and into the parking lot.

She rose and took a step toward the chapel door, concerned for her friend Anita. A flash of light burst from under the door and a second later was gone. The chapel door opened and Luke charged out, bumping into Susan on his way to the side door. Susan had just regained her balance when she heard Anita squealing with delight.

She looked up to find Anita running out of the chapel. Anita stopped and looked at the woman in front of her. "Susan, is that you?" Susan opened her arms and Anita rushed into them and clung to her. Through the waterfall of tears and the excited, shrill pitch of her friend's voice, Susan could barely make out the four words that Anita repeated again and again: "I can see you. I can see you!"

Susan wrapped her arms tightly around Anita.

"I can see you!"

Reverend James walked out of the chapel; his exhausted face beamed with joy for the gift he was able to give these women.

They included him in their embrace.

He smiled when they started jumping up and down, reveling in the absolute joy of the moment.

Reverend James looked through the tangle of arms and hair, to the door the photographer and Luke had gone through only seconds earlier, and his smile faded.

CHAPTER 24

David, the photographer, had the trunk of his Hyundai open and was putting his camera and lens back in their respective cases. Luke stormed up to the man in a panic.

"Hey, wait a minute, man. You can't go runnin' off like that. What about my interview?"

David didn't bother to look up. "Look, I didn't believe this story when I got it. I believe it even less now."

"Then why did you come here at all?"

"Because, my boss told me to." David closed the trunk and attempted to walk around Luke to get in his vehicle, but Luke stepped sideways to block his path.

"Then he believes it, right?"

David reached into his pocket and pulled out a little black stun gun. The unit crackled with electricity when he pressed the button. "That's your first and last warning, Luke. Get out of my way, or I'll tase your ass." David lit up the unit again, and Luke jumped out of the way. The photographer walked around the car in love with his power.

Luke pleaded. "Come back inside, man—that woman can see."

David opened the car door. "I'm sure she can." A sardonic grin spread across his face. "As a matter of fact, I'm going to quote you on that."

"What about my money?"

"For what?"

"For the story!" Luke was terrified they weren't going to run the story. "You are going to print the story, aren't you?"

David showed Luke the taser, just to remind him who was in charge. "Oh, we'll run the story. You'll get your name in the paper." David plopped into the driver's seat and swung his feet into the car. He looked up into Luke's eyes. "Money? No." He slammed the door shut and put his arm out the open window.

Luke yelled at him. "Fine! Good. Go ahead—somebody will believe it."

David laughed out loud. "Our readers believe anything!" The car sputtered to life, and he shouted out the window. "The story will be out in less than a week."

David put the car in gear and pulled away. He smiled when he thought about the two-hundred-dollar check in his pocket with Luke's name on it. When he gave it back to his editor, he'd get fifty bucks in addition to the money for the story. It was so easy. *People are so stupid,* he thought.

Luke watched David drive away, and with him went his dreams of the Oprah appearance, the two hundred dollars, and his name in the paper. Dejected, he walked across the lot to the side door of the church, his mind already scheming, trying to dream up another way to make money.

***

The Healing of Reverend James

A black BMW 740Li rounded the corner at the far end of the lot. Tony was driving and, as usual, Raymond sat beside him in the front seat. Jesus Juarez was in the back seat, as usual. The three men were laughing until, simultaneously, they spotted Luke. Tony stopped the car right in the middle of the street, his mouth open in disbelief.

"Don't stop in the middle of the street, you idiot," Jesus snapped. "Pull over!"

Tony moved the car curbside and parked. The three men watched Luke enter the side door of the church.

Raymond made the unfortunate choice to talk first—unfortunate for him, anyway. "Isn't that Luke Jones?" Brilliant he was not.

Jesus rewarded the observation with a rap on Raymond's head. He used his right hand where he kept a large ruby ring turned around with the stone toward his palm. It added a little extra pain to reward stupid behavior. "No shit, asshole." Then Jesus focused his venom on Tony and ignored Raymond's yelp. "What the hell is going on here? You told me you did the job."

Tony turned to look at Jesus. "We did!"

Raymond rubbed his head and turned around as well. "I held him down myself, Boss."

"Are you telling me he is walking around on broken kneecaps? Is that the bullshit you're gonna fly with?"

Raymond and Tony had been here before. All they could do was wait to see what Jesus would decide to do. Tony was hoping it wouldn't be a boat ride out onto Lake Erie. Jesus didn't enjoy fishing, but he had fed the fishes in the past.

"I don't know what the hell is going on here." Jesus reached under his suit coat and withdrew his nine millimeter Smith and Wesson semi-automatic and waved it back and forth in front of the men's faces. "You're going to pay Luke another visit, and I'm coming with you. If he's still walking after that—you two won't be."

CHAPTER 25

Father Kirk sat behind his desk in the church office. "James, I just don't know what to say."

"Just say you believe me. You've got the proof!"

The priest searched for the right words and avoided eye contact. "There's no doubt that Anita and Susan are...better, but there's really no concrete proof that…"

"Better?" Reverend James was incredulous. More than that, he was mad. "Better? Patrick you have the proof, and you know it, but that's not what we're really talking about, is it?"

Father Kirk breathed a heavy sigh and stared at the floor. He took his time and chose his words carefully. "James, I wish I could speak just for myself." He looked into the eyes of his longtime friend. "If I were to publicly say that people could be healed by— by the laying on of hands, the Vatican would be on the phone with me tomorrow. They would want to know how; they would want to know who, and the next question would be, 'What do you mean, he's not a Catholic?'" The priest hated hearing the words come out of his mouth, but it was the truth.

For his whole life, religion had been a wonderful thing for Father Kirk. He had dedicated his life to helping other people. The Catholic Church was incredibly wonderful on so many levels. The lives that had been helped had numbered in the billions over the years. Lately, all that good had been overshadowed by a pedophile scandal and a church cover-up. While it didn't represent the vast majority of priests, it had hurt many children over many years, and the publicity had brought the Church humiliation and shame.

The new pope, Pope Francis, was doing a fabulous job of restoring much of the Church's integrity. The last thing the Vatican wanted was more fodder for the press. He didn't even want to consider Bishop Walters' response.

"I'm sorry, my friend." The look in Father Kirk's eyes was sincere.

"Okay, Patrick." Reverend James' church was loosely affiliated with other Baptist churches in the tri-state area of New York, Pennsylvania, and Ohio. There was no structure or entity like the Vatican, however. "Maybe this is the way He wants it."

The two friends sat in thoughtful silence. Father Kirk was the first to speak.

"James, you look exhausted."

The preacher nodded. He felt exhausted. He asked the question that had been growing in his mind: "Why me?"

Father Kirk gave his friend the only answer he had. "That, Reverend James, you will have to ask God."

CHAPTER 26

Luke Jones paced the floor between the coffee table and the couch in his living room. The television blared with the sounds of *America's Funniest Home Videos*. His mind was far too busy to enjoy it. He stopped and talked to the ceiling.

"I'm sitting on a gold mine and I can't cash in. Why me?"

Luke changed gears and thought about the conversation he'd had with Reverend James after they had healed Anita and the reporter left. The preacher had lectured him for twenty minutes about respecting people's privacy and not using their gift for financial gain. Normally, Luke would have told him to stick it where the sun don't shine and walked out of there, but the preacher still had the twenty dollars he was promised, and he needed that money. Finally, when Reverend James decided he needed to go see his priest friend, Father Kirk, he had coughed up the cash.

The bottle of Black Velvet was in the kitchen, but Luke, to his surprise, wanted to figure something out about this healing stuff before he started drinking. He had no intention of letting the preacher dissuade him from a financial opportunity like this one. He started talking to the ceiling again.

"Do you know what people would pay to be healed?" Luke imagined posting information about the healing online. He had never gotten involved in Facebook, or tweeting or anything like that, but with this kind of potential, he could learn. He started to dream of people jetting into Buffalo from all over the world, fighting—or better yet, paying—for the chance to be first.

He needed the proof. No one else could be there beside the two of them and the person being healed. *There has to be a way!*

The scorched real estate that was Luke's brain was invaded by an extra loud burst of laughter from the television. Luke watched the replay of a middle-aged man riding a bicycle off a ramp and missing the landing. The man went over the handle bars and landed, face first, in a rosebush.

Luke winced and talked to the ceiling yet again. "You see what I mean? Some idiot is going to get ten thousand dollars just because he sent in a video of…" Luke froze. "Videotape! I've got one of those!"

Luke dashed to the closet that was in between the kitchen and the living room. He swung the door open and dug in. Plastic bags and a broom flew out onto the floor, then a dustpan, empty beer cans, and a bunch of moldy McDonalds bags.

"AHA!" he shouted with glee. Luke held outdated technology in his hand. It was one of the first miniature video cameras that used a mini VHS tape. He punched the button to open the door and prayed it was still in there. To his amazement, it was. He dug in the closet a little deeper and found the wires that would allow him to play back the tape on his television, and there they were. He couldn't believe his luck.

Luke carefully placed the videotape machine up on the shelf, along with the cord. He kicked the other items back into the closet and closed the door. He would worry about how to set it up in the chapel later. Right now, it was time to celebrate, and he had a brand new bottle of Black Velvet. Life couldn't get any sweeter than that.

He retrieved a glass from the sink and rinsed it out. A little ice from the fridge and he filled the vessel up with the alcohol. He took his drink and walked into the living room to catch a buzz while watching his favorite show. That was when the party ended.

Raymond opened Luke's front door and walked in, followed by Tony and Jesus. Luke stopped just inside the living room and watched Raymond and Tony split up, Raymond behind the couch and Tony in between the couch and television. Jesus, baseball bat in hand, blocked the front door. Luke knew that he should run, but his body appeared to have grown roots, fertilized in fear. He was unable to make the transition to the flight instinct fast enough to have a chance of making it out the back door.

Raymond's fist pounded Luke's jaw, and the ice and alcohol flew everywhere when Luke's head smashed into the corner of the hallway. Luke's eyes rolled back in his head, and his knees buckled. He started to slide down the wall, but Raymond grabbed him by his sweatshirt and held him up.

Tony jumped in and grasped Luke's ankles and the two men lifted the dazed man and put him face up on the coffee table.

"This time, we're going to break a lot more than just your knees," Raymond barked.

Raymond stretched out his arm towards his boss and caught the bat that Jesus tossed him. Tony held on to Luke's ankles, and Raymond brought the bat down hard into Luke's ribcage. The sound of the crunch pleased Raymond. Luke's ribs snapped under the force of the blow, and he writhed in pain.

Luke brought his arms up to try to block the next blow and his left forearm broke when the bat came down again. He screamed in agony, only staying on the coffee table because of Tony's grip on his ankles. Raymond smashed both Luke's kneecaps in rapid succession and looked to his boss.

Jesus watched the television, laughing at the montage of men being hit in the groin. He felt Raymond's gaze and turned his attention back to the man who whimpered and groaned on the coffee table. After he had surveyed the situation, Jesus made a flicking motion with his hands. Raymond understood, picked up his foot, and snap-kicked Luke off the coffee table and onto the floor, just as Tony let go of Luke's ankles.

The room filled with the sounds of Luke's shrieks. Tony looked at Jesus and waited. Luke's cries died to a whimper as he laid there half on his side and half on his stomach.

Raymond leaned over and shouted at Luke. "Get up and walk now, bitch!"

The corners of Jesus' mouth curled up into a smile, and he nodded at his enforcers. Without a word, the three men turned and left.

Through the pain-filled haze, Luke heard the men leave. He was in and out of consciousness and lost track of time. When he came to for the third or fourth time, his television show was over, and he recognized the programming from the eight pm to nine pm hour. *Maybe I won't die, after all,* he thought.

He knew he needed Reverend James, and fast. Trouble was, the preacher's phone number was taped to the refrigerator. Luke knew he could never make it over there. His home phone had been disconnected for months, anyway. *Damn it,* he thought, *I should have gotten one of those free government phones that Jennifer told me about.* He thought about his three girls and wondered if they would even care when they found out he was dead. It was the last thought Luke had before he passed out.

CHAPTER 27

Luke heard his name being called and knew his time of reckoning had come. He expected the devil and his minions to have deep, scary voices like he had heard in the movies of his youth. He heard his name again, the voice soft and lilting. Somewhere in Luke's mind was a thought that he had heard the voice before. It sounded familiar. It sounded like—Jennifer!

Luke opened his eyes and found the mother of his two children in his face. "Thank God!" Jennifer cried. "Luke, can you hear me?"

It took a minute for the words to make sense to Luke. His addled brain tried to figure out if this was a dream or a vision. Then he saw his television, and the memory of what had happened to him came rushing back, along with the pain.

"Jennifer?"

Jennifer reached into her pocket and pulled out her government-issued phone. "I'm going to get you an ambulance, Luke."

"No!"

Jennifer was startled by the strength of Luke's reply, and hesitated.

"Reverend James!" Luke groaned. "Phone number—fridge." Luke whimpered with every breath, the broken ribs sending pain shooting through his brain. Every little movement amplified the pain, and it echoed throughout his body. He had to make Jennifer understand that he needed the preacher.

"Luke, you need to get to the hospital! I'm calling 911."

Jennifer brought the phone up, and Luke used his one good arm to slap it out of her hand, as he screamed at her. "No!"

"Luke, what the hell are you doing? I'm trying to help you."

Luke's eyes were glazed, and he fought through the excruciating pain and forced the words through his gritted teeth. "Reverend James—fridge!"

Jennifer stared into Luke's eyes. She watched him wrestle the agony to keep his eyes on hers. There were tears streaming down his face, and his eyes pleaded with her. "Please?" Luke managed to croak out.

Jennifer couldn't remember the last time she had heard that word come out of Luke's mouth, except for right after he asked to borrow money.

"Fine," she said, "I'll call the preacher." Jennifer retrieved her phone and walked to the refrigerator, talking as she went. "If you die because you wouldn't let me call an ambulance, it's your own damn fault." She punched in the number.

***

It was just over twelve minutes after Jennifer called the preacher that he burst through Luke's front door. He spotted Jennifer hovering over Luke and went to her side immediately. "Dear, Lord." Reverend James could see that Luke was in real trouble. He needed to move fast. He turned to Jennifer.

"Thanks for calling, Jennifer. I'm sorry to do this to you, but I'm going to need you to wait outside."

Jennifer wasn't going to be brushed aside so easily. "I'm not going outside, Reverend." Jennifer pulled her phone out of her back pocket. "I'm going to call an ambulance like I should have done in the first place."

"He's not going to need an ambulance, Jennifer."

Jennifer misinterpreted the comment. "Oh, God! He's going to die?"

Reverend James spoke fast to keep Jennifer calm. "Luke is not going to die, Jennifer."

She stared at him.

"I'm going to heal him."

Jennifer's mind raced with the memory of the conversation she'd had with Luke about the previous healings. "What? Great—you're just as crazy as he is."

The preacher nodded. "Yes, I am." Reverend James took Jennifer's hand and pulled her to her feet. "I just need you to wait outside." He pushed Jennifer toward the door.

"He tried to tell me he was your witness—and that you could heal people—but I don't believe him."

"That's fine. Now, please just wait outside."

"I'm the one who called you. Why are you trying to get rid of me?"

"It won't work if you are in here. You'll just have to trust me on this. Luke needs me—right now!"

The Healing of Reverend James

He saw the fear in her eyes when he forcefully shoved her out the door. "Don't panic. In two minutes, everything will be fine." He closed the door in Jennifer's face and rushed back to Luke.

He heard Jennifer scream through the door, "I'm calling 911!"

Reverend James couldn't believe it had been just this morning they had healed Anita. It felt like weeks ago. He had spent most of the day after the healing trying to calm down from Luke's attempt at publicity. It was true he hadn't thought about what they would do about finding people to heal. It was all too soon. There were five or six people in his congregation who could use his help, but what then?

***

When he and Maya had gone to lunch together earlier that day, he had asked her opinion. Maya was hesitant, to say the least, but after some coaxing she spoke her mind. He was almost sorry he asked.

"I don't like it one bit!" Maya said.

Reverend James was taken aback by the comment. The strength of Maya's conviction surprised him.

"Wow. I have to admit, I wasn't expecting that."

"Well, you asked," Maya replied. The two sat in silence for what seemed an eternity.

"Why do you feel that way?"

189

Maya looked the preacher straight in the eyes and responded. "There are a couple of reasons, James. First off, you are not God."

"I know that," he managed. "Don't you think I know that?"

"You sure you want my opinion on this, James?"

The preacher nodded. "Yes, yes I do." He sat back in the booth and tried to hide the anxiety that threatened to take hold.

"Most people that have ever claimed to be healers are some kind of snake-oil salesmen who prey upon the sick for money. Have you considered that?"

"But that's not what we're doing here," he argued. "You know that."

"Not now, perhaps not ever. Are you sure you never will?"

Reverend James was speechless. He wanted to tell her he would never do a thing like that. When he thought about it, it *had* occurred to him that some grateful person whom he had healed might make a large donation to his church. Money was always a concern for the church. Was that the same thing?

Maya let him off the hook. "I'm sure you're not planning on selling your healing services to the highest bidder, James. I know you better than that. My concern is the big picture."

"What do you mean?" he asked.

"You said your vision of your great-grandfather said there would be three conditions on this gift you were given. You've already discovered two. What's the last one?"

Reverend James shrugged. "I don't know."

"Just look at what you do know." Maya continued. "The person that apparently has to be there when you heal people is Luke Jones. Luke Jones! This is a good thing?"

"I don't know. I—I just don't know."

"You almost strangled the man to death, James. I'm thinking that is a problem."

"We're past that now."

"Another condition: the healing doesn't work if anyone else is present. What does that mean?"

The preacher looked confused. "I'm not sure what you are getting at?"

"What I'm trying to say is you don't even know the other condition on your...gift. You don't know what the conditions mean that you do know about." Maya leaned in to him. "You also don't know what the ramifications of these healings will be. Frankly, that concerns me the most."

Reverend James was lost in thought. He had been so concerned with figuring out *how* to make the healing work, he hadn't considered anything else.

"I haven't even thought of that, Maya. How would I even know what the ramifications are?"

"You won't. I'm just saying that before you go announcing this to the world, I think it would be wise to at least consider what might happen, and be prepared, if you can."

***

Reverend James looked down at Luke's broken body. He knew he could heal this man, but he hesitated just the same. This would be the second time he had healed Luke and the second time today he had healed someone. Ironic that out of four healings, only three people were healed. Luke Jones would represent fifty percent of those healings.

The preacher knew Jennifer was waiting outside. He decided she had waited long enough. He clasped his hands together against his chest and gently laid them on Luke.

Reverend James watched the light shoot out of his hands and cover Luke's body. The light soaked in and then shot off in all directions and disappeared. Then everything went dark.

***

Jennifer was standing outside of Luke's house and had waited to call 911. At first, when she heard Luke's terrified screams, she froze. She heard it again through the door, Luke was screaming her name. She opened the door and rushed into the living room. Her mind told her what she saw was not possible. There was Luke, alive and vibrant, no broken bones, no blood, nothing. Luke was sprawled across Reverend James' body. He was bouncing up and down like a bull rider in a rodeo. The preacher was having a grand mal seizure, and the convulsions were violent.

"Jennifer, help me!" Luke shrieked.

Jennifer's training kicked in. "Put him on his side. Put him on his side!" Jennifer ran to Luke and helped him roll the seizing preacher on his side. Foam bubbled out of the preacher's mouth, and his eyes were fluttering in his head.

"Shouldn't we put something in his mouth so he doesn't bite his tongue?" Luke asked.

"No, he could choke on it," she replied. "Just keep him on his side. I'm calling 911."

The preacher's seizure subsided, and Luke took a breath. Jennifer, phone in hand, stared at Luke.

"What?" he asked.

Jennifer was wrestling with her belief structure. What she was looking at was impossible. "You were telling me the truth," she muttered.

Luke screamed. "Just get an ambulance here!"

Jennifer dialed 911 and fed the proper information to the emergency operator. She hung up the phone and stared at Luke. He cradled the preacher in his arms and held him up on his side.

"I don't understand what happened, Luke. Reverend James said you would be fine, and you are, but what happened to him?"

"I don't know, Jennifer. I don't know."

Jennifer placed her hands on the preacher's wrist and was pleased to find a strong pulse.

"I need to ask you something, Jennifer." Luke continued.

Jennifer held up her wait-a-minute finger and continued to count. Seventy-two beats per minute. That was great. She looked at Luke. "What is it, Luke?"

"What are you doing here?" The question had been on Luke's mind since he first realized it was Jennifer kneeling beside him. He had been busy trying not to die at the time, and hadn't gotten around to asking.

"Tony," she said.

"Tony!"

"Yeah, y'know," she continued, "Scarface." They had jokingly called him that since the car accident. Not to his face, of course.

Luke was shocked. "He *did* this to me," he shouted.

"All I can tell you is he was afraid to call 911. He thought Jesus would be able to track the call back to him." Luke just sat there in stunned silence, so she continued. "He took a heck of a risk. He told Jesus he just wanted to go see an old girlfriend to see if he could get laid." Jennifer answered the question before Luke asked it. "No, nothing happened. He just told me I needed to hurry, that he thought Raymond had hurt you too bad. Then he left."

So Luke owed Tony for helping him. *He might have saved my life.* The thought had barely occurred to Luke when Reverend James began another seizure. He held onto the preacher; Jennifer hung on as well. In the distance, they could hear an approaching siren. They hoped it would arrive in time.

CHAPTER 28

The hospital room was filled with so many flowers that it looked like a greenhouse. Reverend James was covered up to his neck with a blanket; only his arms and head were exposed. An IV hung from the rolling IV pole and dripped normal saline solution into the preacher's vein to keep him hydrated. He found himself in a private room.

Reverend James had been moved there partially due to the crowded and unavailable semi-private rooms, but mostly due to the amount of flowers he'd received. It also helped that one of his nurses on second shift was a member of his church and had influenced the Director of Nursing when they were deciding where to put everybody. The late-September nights had turned cold, and that always seemed to fill hospital beds.

Mary Matthews was sitting in the chair closest to the bed. She had a Bible in one hand and her son's hand in the other. Next to her, with a chair between them, sat Luke Jones, his face buried in his hands. Mary would not have been sitting this close to Luke if she could have read his mind.

Luke had a newspaper tucked under his arm, and his mind was busy feeling sorry for himself. He could almost smell the money that the healings would have rained down upon them, but here he sat with an unconscious preacher and a headache.

It had been three days since Reverend James had been brought to WCA Hospital. They couldn't find anything wrong with him—except that he was comatose. CT scans, MRIs, and various poking and prodding had all revealed the same thing: nothing. He was sleeping, and he wouldn't wake up.

The preacher had had three seizures; at least, that's what the doctors concluded. Luke had witnessed the first two, but not the last. The medical professionals were as confused as anybody else at their inability to find the cause. They had even stopped his anti-convulsants yesterday and put him under observation. There was no change. Luke felt like he had the winning lottery ticket, and he couldn't cash it in.

Mary Matthews was struggling with some powerful thoughts as well. Just one seat away from her was the man who had killed her daughter-in-law. She had prayed for forgiveness for Luke—at least, for God to forgive him. But now that he was involved with her son and this healing business, she had to face her anger up close and personal.

She believed God had a plan; she always had. When God had taken her husband, Quentin, on that snowy April day, she had known it was part of a plan that she could not understand. She was able to accept that situation and move on. Maybe it was the alcohol: Luke's being drunk and running the stop sign. Maybe it was the fact that she had watched the event happen right in front of her own eyes. She could still hear the sounds from that day. She could smell the oil and gasoline. The memory of seeing it happen was definitely the worse.

She knew she had to forgive Luke. It was her Christian duty. But did she have to sit next to him? The sense of foreboding that had begun when she first heard her son tell of his vision in the chapel was growing. She could also tell that Luke was up to something. She wasn't sure what, but something. She could see it in his eyes, and it made her wary.

Dear Lord, she began, *please help me to accept your will, whether I understand it or not. Please help me to forgive Luke Jones. Please help me forgive Luke Jones.* Mary prayed it a third time, desperate to let go of the anger and hate. *Please help me forgive Luke Jones!*

The movement of her right hand startled Mary, and she jumped in her chair. She glanced up to see her son looking into her eyes. A smile burst onto her face and tears welled up in her eyes. She said a silent thank-you to God. "Good afternoon, James."

Reverend James opened his mouth to speak, but his mouth was dry, and he could only cough. Mary turned to Luke, who had risen from his seat when he'd heard Mary talk to her son.

"Luke, would you please get a cup of water for James?" Mary pointed to the rolling table on the other side of the bed.

Luke moved too quickly and kicked the leg of the bed. He made it to the water pitcher without further incident. He filled the paper cup with water and handed it to the preacher. He opened his mouth to speak, but the look on Mary's face changed his mind. He was glad he had quickly given the cup to the preacher because he was certain the water in the cup would have turned to ice in his hand.

Mary used the remote to raise the back of the bed, and James drank greedily, handing the cup to Luke for a refill . He turned to his mother.

"Hi, Momma," he croaked.

Luke handed him the cup again, and the preacher stared at him for a moment and back at his mother. The fact that these two people were in the same room together was something of a miracle in itself. His thirst interrupted the thought, and he drained the second cup as well.

Mary took charge, not that there was any doubt. "Take it easy, James. It's been a while since you've had anything to eat or drink, except by IV, anyway."

The preacher looked at his IV and became aware of the enormous amount of flowers that filled the space.

"How long have I been here?" he asked.

Luke forgot who was in charge. "Three days." He was rewarded for his answer with matching glares from both of them.

"Three days?" Reverend James looked distraught. "I've been laying here for three days?"

"Yes, you have, James." His mother rose and looked down at him. "Don't you worry about that, James. What do you say we get you something to eat? You must be hungry."

The preacher shook his head. "No, I'm not hungry, but—" Reverend James looked confused. "How did I get here—what happened?"

Mary turned to Luke. "Go ahead, Luke, you were there."

The Healing of Reverend James

Luke ran through the events at his house and took more time when he got to the part where he woke up to find the preacher having a grand mal seizure. He left out the part about Tony contacting Jennifer; the fewer people who had that information, the better.

Reverend James pondered the scenario Luke had presented. He remembered the frantic phone call from Jennifer and rushing over to Luke's house. He remembered asking Jennifer to wait outside and kneeling next to Luke. There was the light from his hands, and then nothing.

"James, now isn't the time to worry about this," Mary said. "We need to get you fed, and I need to let the nurse know that you're awake. You need rest. Ever since this healing business started, you've been exhausted. Take it easy."

Luke took a chance that he'd be allowed to speak. He had some exciting news that he wanted to share. "We need you healthy, Reverend," Luke said. "We've got work to do."

"I'm just trying to figure out why I'm in the hospital." Reverend James looked at each of them in turn. "I mean, it's not like it was the first time I healed someone…" He stopped and grew still, a worried look on his face.

"What is it, James?" Mary asked.

The preacher just looked at her, unable to speak.

Luke walked around the bed to the chair he had just gotten up from and grabbed the newspaper he had left there. He tossed it into the preacher's lap. "Check that out, Reverend, we're famous."

"Luke!" Mary was furious.

Reverend James looked down at the paper in front of him. The headline read: BAPTIST PREACHER MAKES THE BLIND SEE. His heart stopped when he recognized the photograph under the headline. It was his church. There was a shot of him kneeling next to Anita in the chapel. It wasn't even the local paper. It was the national rag sheet that always spouted off about finding Bigfoot and people being abducted by aliens.

"I got my name in the paper." Luke pointed to the article. "People are coming to the church every day."

"Luke, not now." Mary tried to stop Luke, who was oblivious to the look of terror on the preacher's face.

"There's already...twenty or so sick people waiting to be healed." Luke looked triumphant.

"Waiting to be healed? What do you mean there are people waiting to be healed?" The preacher's eyes looked like those of a frightened horse.

"James, honey, you shouldn't be dealing with that right now."

"Mother, please."

The look he gave Mary did its job. She was quiet.

"Luke," the preacher demanded, "what do you mean there are people waiting to be healed?"

Luke finally realized the preacher was upset. "In your church...there's a bunch of people waiting to be healed."

Reverend James' mind raced with pictures of the sick and dying filling the pews of his church. The fear changed to dread as the thought matured. The pieces of the puzzle had suddenly come together, and the preacher was shell-shocked. He looked into his mother's eyes for help.

"What's the matter, James. I don't like the look on your face." Mary had flashbacks to the day they had buried John. Her son had had that same look in his eyes then.

The preacher looked at Luke and back to his mother. "You don't understand, do you?"

Luke and Mary were still. The tension had permeated the room in an instant. "What, child?" Mary managed to get out.

"The people at the church—He's going to make me..." Tears began to roll down the preacher's cheeks.

"I'll be there to help, Reverend James." Luke thought he understood. He didn't have a clue.

"I healed Anita and you on the same day," the preacher began, "and I end up in here for three days, maybe four by the time I get out. They didn't find anything wrong with me, did they, Momma?"

Mary shook her head. "No. The tests were all negative, but..."

"It's the third condition on my gift of healing," the preacher continued. "I can only heal one person a day or I risk killing myself."

The preacher was certain he was right. He could feel it in his bones, and the thought crushed him. He waited and saw that they still did not understand. He could tell by the looks on their faces. It was even worse than that, and Reverend James knew it. It all made sense now; the preacher was absolutely certain he was correct. "I won't be able to heal them all, the people at the church—or anywhere. God is going to make me choose—who lives—and who dies."

CHAPTER 29

Reverend James walked in the side door of his church and couldn't believe what he saw; more than two dozen groups of people camped out in the pews. A few people were by themselves, but mostly there were groups of two or three. There was even what appeared to be three generations from the same Asian family that took up half of two rows of pews in the southwest corner.

A few people noticed his arrival and recognized Reverend James from his photograph in the paper. They whispered and nudged the people in their group, and in just seconds half the people were staring at the preacher. In less than a minute the entire room was silently gazing upon the man they had come to see: the Healer.

Luke Jones walked in the side door and didn't hesitate to annoy Reverend James. "See, first day back and you already have a following."

The preacher glared at Luke and without a word, turned and walked into the chapel. Every eye in the place tracked Reverend James and watched him disappear when the chapel door closed. The group immediately turned and stared at Luke. Luke headed for the chapel and thought of something clever to tell the group. "Uh—we'll be right back, folks." Luke bolted for the chapel door.

***

Luke scooted through the chapel door and bounded over to Reverend James, who sat in his normal place in the second row. He stared at his great-grandfather's cross.

Luke interrupted his thoughts. "We gonna heal somebody today, or not?"

Reverend James sighed and kept his eyes on the cross. "How do I choose, Luke?"

"You asking me?" Luke was stunned by the question.

The preacher looked at Luke and then back at the cross. "At least I can get an answer from you."

Luke wasn't expecting to have to deal with this, but he saw the troubled look on Reverend James' face and realized he would have to come up with something.

"Well, if it were me—I'd try to figure who needs it the most." Luke liked the way that sounded and congratulated himself for being so clever.

The victory was short-lived. "Do you know who needs it the most, Luke?"

Luke's brain scrambled for a response. "I mean...figure out who it would do the most good to heal."

"How do I do that?" The preacher wasn't taunting Luke; he was serious.

Luke couldn't believe how badly this conversation made his head hurt. He couldn't come up with an answer, so he shrugged his shoulders and sat in the pew opposite Reverend James and was quiet.

Reverend James turned his attention back to the cross. His mind wandered to that fateful day when he had torn it from the wall and broken it. Right now, he was kind of wishing he had made a different choice. Perhaps this was all just a bad dream, and he would wake up and he could—do what? What did he wish he had done instead? That was the trouble with life and choices. It was easier to second guess yourself after making a choice and seeing the result of that action. Harder still was living with the outcomes of those decisions—especially the bad ones. Outcomes were easy to live with if everything worked out the way you wanted them to, but how often did that happen, really? Was being given the power to heal people a bad outcome? Not for Susan and Anita—at least, not that he was aware of. It was good for them, he hoped.

Reverend James realized he had allowed his mind to ramble on about things beyond his control. He had to live with the outcomes of the decisions he had already made. *How could I have known that I would be given this healing gift when I broke that cross,* he thought? *I didn't ask for this—Or, did I?*

He allowed the memory of that day into his head, the memory of his words to God just before he had torn the cross off the wall. *How dare you take them from me?* The words filled his memory and rocked his soul. He had dared to judge God, and now he had a power that didn't feel like it was a gift at all.

Reverend James shook his head and refocused his thoughts. He wasn't going to be able to help anyone if he didn't figure out how. He had always told the members of his congregation that no one could change the past. The only power any person had was in the moment, right now. He wanted to make a decision that he would be proud of tomorrow. That gave him his answer, he realized. These people who waited in his church were intimately involved in this, too, and they deserved the truth. They needed to know.

He turned to Luke. "We have to tell them, Luke."

"Tell them about what?"

"One person a day."

"Oh—yeah."

Reverend James rose and stepped out of the pew. "I'm going to take your advice. I'll have to talk to each person and find out what I can about them." Reverend James searched the pocket of his suit coat and found it empty. He would need his great-grandfather's Bible in his pocket for this chore. He made a mental note to retrieve it before he began.

"After I'm done talking to them...I'll have to decide."

Luke rose and stood in the pew. "Kind of like winning a contest, huh?"

Reverend James was enraged by the heartless comment and struggled to keep from screaming. "Don't you ever talk like that again!"

"What did I say?"

"This is not a contest!" The preacher hissed through his clenched jaw.

"I didn't mean..."

Reverend James overpowered him. "You didn't mean what, Luke? These are people's lives we're talking about here, not the daily number."

The preacher went to the door of the chapel, partly to make sure no one was listening, but mostly so he didn't have to look at Luke's face. He stared through the window and saw that the people were pretty much where he had last seen them. He tried to get a grip on his runaway emotions. That always proved difficult whenever Luke was around.

"You sure you're up for this, Reverend?" Luke stepped out of the pew and glared at the preacher's back.

Reverend James nodded his head and answered without turning around. "Yes, I think so. It'll just take some time."

"That's okay," Luke answered. "I have some stuff to take care of, anyway."

The preacher whirled around. "No photographers, Luke!"

Luke was a little too quick to agree. "No photographers."

"No one!"

"I promise." Luke crossed his heart and was the picture of innocence.

Reverend James' eyes drilled into him. He didn't trust Luke, but he couldn't perceive any issues at that moment. The preacher turned and walked out the chapel door.

Luke turned away from the window, and a knowing smile spread across his face.

CHAPTER 30

Reverend James retrieved his great-grandfather's Bible from its place in his desk drawer. He kept his hand on it while he gathered together the people who were hoping to be healed. With the Bible in his pocket, his confidence was strengthened, but nothing could have prepared him for the looks on their faces when he told them the conditions on his gift.

The younger people recovered quickly, the hope returning to their faces in just moments. The older people, however, seemed to realize their dilemma immediately and could not hide their fear and disappointment.

One elderly white woman approached him right after his announcement and explained that she was leaving. He tried to convince her to stay and be interviewed, but she could not be swayed. She calmly stated that, with this new information, it was apparent to her that she should defer to others in the group whose need and viability made her decision simple. She wished him well and left.

Viability? A nice way of saying she knew she would not be among the first to be chosen due to her age, and she accepted that fact. The preacher was relieved to have one less person to consider, but humbled and distraught that he knew her foresight to be true. *How am I going to be able to pick just one of these people?* He asked himself. For a moment, the terrible, awful choice grabbed a hold of his heart and mind and made it hard to breathe. Then he remembered something hopeful. Tomorrow he could choose another, and another the day after that. In three weeks, he could heal them all.

When Reverend James started thinking in terms of weeks, another thought paraded into his brain to add to the confusion. Today was Monday. He had spent four and a half days in the hospital. Now he had all these people in his church. He was also going to have to come up with a plan to accommodate those new facts. *How did Reverend Washington deal with all these people during services yesterday?* He hadn't mentioned it when they'd talked last night, and Maya didn't say anything, either. The preacher made a mental note to discuss it with her later today when he was…finished.

Reverend Washington had been in a hurry to leave last night and looked a bit uncomfortable when they had spoken. Reverend James had wanted to discuss what was going on with him, but it had been clear that his friend had just wanted to get back to Buffalo. At least that was what he'd said. So the preacher had thanked him for helping again, and they'd said their goodbyes.

Reverend James knew that it was up to him to solve these issues. Exactly what he was going to do would have to wait; he needed to make a choice, and it was time to get started.

He had already assessed that no one in the room was in danger of passing away today from their issues, although some were obviously quite ill. He decided to start with a young black man who was seated right in front of him. He looked familiar. *This boy looks like he is John's age;* the preacher thought, and then quickly corrected himself. *The age John would be today if he were still—here.*

It was a little over three weeks since John's burial, but it felt like a lifetime ago. Reverend James knew he couldn't allow those emotions to grab hold of him, or he would never get through what he had to do today. He took a deep breath and extended his hand to the young man in front of him.

"Hello, my name is Reverend Matthews."

The young man extended a shaky hand to him. "I'm Trevor. I'm from your church."

***

Luke looked through the side door of the church and saw the preacher was busy interviewing the people in the pews. He opened the door and headed for the chapel. He carried a worn backpack over his shoulder and tried to appear as nonchalant as possible. When the chapel door closed behind him, he breathed a sigh of relief and went to work.

He set the backpack on the front pew of the chapel and pulled out the video camera he had brought from his house. He had already scouted the chapel for a clandestine location and turned and saw that nothing had changed since then. On each side of the altar, about six feet above the floor, was a shelf. On each shelf were two plants; a spider plant was toward the front, and a Christmas cactus was toward the back. It was time to see if the spider plant would conceal the camera from view as well as he hoped it would.

Luke placed the machine on the shelf and tucked it behind the plant, tight against the wall. He walked to the back of the chapel to check it out. The leaves of the plant concealed the camera quite well, but not well enough. Luke knew he was only going to get one shot at this. If the preacher spotted the camera, he was finished.

When Luke had originally thought up the idea to use the video camera, he had already concocted an excuse, should he get caught. He was going to tell Reverend James that his girlfriend didn't believe his stories about the healings, so he was going to show her proof. His mind had come up with the scheme while he was putting everything back in the closet that night. Then he got busted up by Tony and Raymond, and Jennifer was there to see him get healed, which blew that excuse. He had to be sure not to blow this chance.

At the hospital, when Reverend James had told him and Mary that he could heal only one person a day, the wind had gone out of Luke's sails. Then he'd had an epiphany. Any commodity or service that had a limited supply was automatically worth more money, right? Not only did the preacher need Luke—he *had* to have him there, or the healings wouldn't work. As far as Luke was concerned, that gave him leverage. If the preacher wanted to heal people, he would have to agree to Luke's plan.

Luke smiled to himself as he walked over to reset the camera. His hands worked on rearranging the plant to better hide it, while his mind danced with the beauty of his scheme. He knew the preacher would put up a fight over charging money to *everyone* who needed to be healed. He was a preacher, and that was what they did: help the poor and all that. So Luke, applying his logic and genius to the plan, came up with what he thought was the perfect compromise. Reverend James would get to pick who got healed one day, and Luke would get to pick who got healed the next. That would result in an alternating schedule of days that would allow Luke to schedule healings for anybody, from anywhere around the world, every other day. Perfect! How could the preacher refuse?

For any of this to work, Luke had to get the video of a healing that he could post online. He didn't know how to convert video to digital, or how to post anything, but he was certain he could find someone who could. They would have to wait to get their money until Luke got his, but that was no problem considering the amount of money Luke knew was possible.

Luke was so busy congratulating himself for his genius that he missed the step down from the altar and almost tumbled into the front pew. At the last moment, he managed to catch himself and save his face. His wrist didn't fare as well, and Luke had to keep from yelling when the pain made it to his brain. He gingerly held his wrist against his stomach and traveled to the back of the chapel to check out the new location for the camera. It was flawless. The leaves of the spider plant beautifully hid the body of the camera.

Now, there was just one more test. Luke pulled the camera off the shelf and turned it on. He put it on the shelf and went to the back of the chapel. He could see the blinking red light through the leaves, but had already considered that. He had duct tape in the backpack that would cover the light.

Luke mimed for the camera, waving and smiling. He only needed to make sure the last two rows near the aisle were in view. He walked from one side of the aisle to the other. Then he walked back and forth along the last two rows of pews. Luke retrieved the camera from its hiding place and hit the rewind button. There was no flip-out display in the aged machine, so Luke looked into the eyepiece to see what he had recorded.

Right away, Luke saw himself walking to the back of the chapel. Moment by moment, his smile grew as he watched the playback. The placement was perfect. He rewound the recorder again and stepped off the altar. He grabbed the duct tape from the backpack and ripped off a small piece. Carefully, he placed the tape over the light and hit the record button. It worked. The blinking red light was invisible.

Luke returned the recorder to the shelf and walked to the front of the chapel. When he was content that the recorder was well hidden, he turned and looked out the window into the church. It looked to Luke like Reverend James had talked to three or four people already, but he had a long way to go. Luke considered going out to help, but decided he couldn't risk it. From his vantage point at the chapel door, he felt he could determine when the preacher was nearing completion of his interviews, and he had to be ready. He only had about thirty minutes of tape available in the recorder, so he had to turn it on as close as possible to the time of the healing. He didn't want to get caught turning it on, nor could he risk it reaching the end of the tape and shutting off while the preacher was still in the room. That would be noisy, and he would be busted. So he would wait. After five years in jail, waiting a couple of hours would a breeze.

Luke stared out the window and daydreamed about the riches that would soon be his. He dreamt of selling the tape to the highest bidder. He would do the talk show circuit and everyone would know his name: lunch with Oprah, dinner with Jimmy Fallon. First he needed the proof. Then the money would come pouring in. Luke forgot that life is what happens to you while you're busy making other plans.

CHAPTER 31

Reverend James had dealt with some horrendously difficult situations in his life before, but nothing he had ever done could have prepared him for this. Each person he talked to was every bit as deserving to be healed as the person before.

The previous events in Reverend James' life that had challenged him were usually, if not always, beyond his control. The death of his wife and the death of his son were two prime examples. Choosing who would be healed tonight, however, was on his shoulders alone—no one else to blame, no one to help, just him.

Two of the people he had already talked to were from his congregation. Neither one was an every-Sunday regular, but that moniker only described half of the people who attended his church. The days of have-to-be-at-church-every-Sunday had been fading since he had been born in the mid-sixties. His church was better off than many of the other denominations in the area.

Father Kirk had reached a point of thirty percent attendance during the worse times of the child abuse scandals that had rocked the Catholic Church. But attendance had rebounded after Pope Francis had been installed. He found himself trying to make a choice based only on the need, but was finding it difficult, if not impossible, to keep his mind focused on that one criterion alone.

Trevor, the first boy he spoke to, had intractable back pain, rare for a person in his early twenties. He was well-spoken and polite, but had the same look of desperation and disbelief he saw in every other person he had spoken with so far. The hardest people to talk to were the people who'd brought their significant others with them, closely followed by those who had their parents with them. They cried, begged, and pleaded for their loved one to be chosen. The people who needed to be healed hardly spoke and seemed embarrassed to have their needs shoved in the preacher's face like that.

He finished with a young married couple. The young wife, Christy Kaufman, had just been diagnosed with breast cancer. She had never smoked and was an athlete in high school and college. She had had her first routine mammogram at twenty-four years of age due to her family history and had been totally surprised when the doctor had told her the results. They had said it was most likely benign, but then had found out they had been wrong. Her breast cancer was virulent and had already metastasized.

She had lost her mother to the same disease just one year earlier and was devastated by the news of her own diagnosis. Her husband was there, as was her father; the latter had actually used a very threatening tone while informing the preacher the he *had* to choose his daughter. Then Dad had broken down into fits of anguished apologies and Reverend James had slipped away while the three of them clung to each other.

It *was* three generations of the Asian family, just as he had supposed when he'd seen them in the far corner of the room earlier. It was the second generation, the mother of the three children who surrounded her who wanted his help. She wore leg braces to help her stand and oxygen to help her breathe. ALS was a horrible degenerative and fatal disease; this attractive thirty-two-year-old mother was entering the later stages. The preacher had experience with the disease. Over the years, he had personally witnessed the progressive decline and death of two of his congregation to this monster.

Her name was Chi Long. Her parents stoically listened as their daughter talked to Reverend James. The only reason Chi's husband hadn't come was the family ran the local Chinese restaurant. They were already short-staffed because the rest of the family was here at his church. The children had skipped school to support their mother. After reassuring them that their mother would be high up on the list, the preacher was able to talk Chi's father into taking the children to school.

Reverend James had already come to the conclusion that he was going to pick the first five people to be healed. The rest would then draw numbers to determine in what order they would be healed. He took a break to go to the restroom, partly because he needed the bathroom break, but mostly because he needed to take a minute to get control of himself and his emotions. Within seconds of making the decision to draw numbers from a hat to determine the order of the healings, he was repulsed and overwhelmed by his choice. He stared into the bathroom mirror and wrestled with his options. *Can I really tell these people that they need to pick their destiny from a hat?*

The preacher viewed his red, tired eyes in the mirror and thanked God no one was on the verge of dying today. He knew that the man in the mirror had gotten him into this mess, and he was the one who had to figure out the solution.

Reverend James decided on one aspect of all this. There was no need for all these people to come to the church every day to wait to be healed. After the order was finalized, he would suggest that they stay home until their day arrived. They would be welcome to come to church for Sunday services if they so desired. All were welcome to attend his church. Until it was their turn, he just thought it would be good for people to continue their everyday lives.

As people do, Reverend James justified his thought processes and was calm and content with his choices when a disturbing thought worked its way into his consciousness. *What am I going to do if more people show up, especially someone in desperate and immediate need?* This rocked his world and kept him in the restroom a couple of minutes longer. What if this whole thing spiraled out of control? There could be hundreds, maybe even thousands of people, once the word got out. He finally came to the conclusion that he would have to make decisions based on what was happening at the time and adjust accordingly. The magnitude of the problem was making him nauseous.

Reverend James forced himself to leave the relative peace and security of the rest room and walked back to face the waiting crowd. There were six or seven people he had to talk to yet, and then it would be time to make a decision. He would take his time and gather his nerve. He pictured the speech he would give these people and prayed they would all remain calm. He knew if they didn't, the anger would be aimed at him. He took a deep breath and trudged back into the pews.

CHAPTER 32

When he'd seen saw the preacher wade back into the crowd, Luke Jones had run to the restroom. That had been over an hour ago. Only moments ago, the preacher had left again and came back with Maya Richards in tow. Maya set down some papers and pencils and a wicker collection basket and left. From the look on her face, Luke figured she was not very happy about what was happening. *Is he going to make them draw numbers from a hat?* Luke marveled at the thought, glad that he made the choice to stay in the chapel. He could sense the time was getting close when he would need to turn on the camera, but not quite yet.

He saw the preacher drawing up some sort of chart, but he couldn't quite make out what it was. It wasn't hard to figure out, however. It was a schedule. The first five rows of the schedule seemed to have been filled in while the rest appeared to be blank. Luke listened through the door as the Reverend James announced the names on the schedule. One by one, Luke watched as groups, or individuals, laughed and cried as their names were read. The preacher made an announcement about people needing to return to their lives and information about the remaining people choosing a number from a basket.

The reaction of the people who had not yet been chosen was remarkably calm. One by one, the individuals came forward and picked a number. It was obvious no one was pleased with the process. The reaction after picking a number ranged from tears to anger, yet all turned and walked back to their seats. Reverend James apologized as he wrote each name down in the appropriate column.

When the last person drew a number, the exhausted crowd gathered for a group prayer with the preacher. The prayer ended. A few people charged out of the church doors, clearly frustrated and angry. The preacher hugged those who would allow it, and Luke knew that was his cue.

He went to the shelf and switched on the power button of the video camera. When he went back to the little window in the chapel door and looked out, Reverend James was giving a hug to a young black man. "Come back tomorrow," Reverend James said. The young man said goodbye to the preacher and left.

Reverend James watched him through the side door. In the distance, he saw Christy Kaufman, the young woman with breast cancer. She would be third.

The only people left in the church were the young Asian woman and what appeared to be her parents. Luke watched Reverend James walk over to the trio and talk for a moment. Then he offered the young woman his arm. He helped her to stand, and they headed for the chapel.

**

Luke held the door open as Reverend James escorted the woman into the chapel. Luke was pleased when Reverend James sat her in the last row on the right side of the chapel. Luke couldn't have picked a better location himself; the camera angle was perfect.

Luke glanced back at the shelf where the camera was, and his heart stopped. Through the leaves, bright as it could be, was a blinking red light. Luke spun around quickly and blocked the preacher's view of the shelf with his body. His mind raced with the knowledge that the duct tape had fallen off the light, but there was nothing he could do about it now. He was going to have to get out of the way so the camera could tape the healing, but that would make it possible for the preacher to see the light.

The preacher turned to Luke. "Join us, Luke." Reverend James turned back to Chi Long.

Luke sat in the pew in front of her and forced himself to fight the instinct to look in the direction of the shelf.

"Mrs. Long," the preacher voiced, "I would like you to remove your braces from your legs."

Chi looked startled and asked, "Why?"

Luke was a little puzzled as well.

"We recently healed a woman that had been in a wheelchair for over two years," the preacher explained. "Her legs were atrophied before the healing, but were fully restored to normal in the process of healing."

Luke remembered and nodded his head. "He's right."

That was good enough for Chi, as she leaned over and struggled to remove the braces. Luke helped her, then took the braces and set them in the pew next to him. Gently, Reverend James removed the oxygen mask. Chi's questioning eyes met the preacher's.

Reverend James answered the question before she asked. "And, no, it doesn't hurt. There will be a bright light, though."

Reverend James brought his hands together and then gently placed them on Chi's leg. Luke had been holding his breath and was relieved when the light shot out of the preacher's hands and was absorbed into the startled women's body. A flash and it was gone.

For a moment, Chi just sat there and stared at the two men. "That was it?" she asked.

"That was it," Reverend James confirmed. "Would you like to see for yourself? I'll walk you out to your parents." She nodded.

Luke jumped to his feet and offered her his hand, which she took. He wasn't just helping her—he was blocking the preacher's line of sight again.

Chi rose to her feet and immediately broke into a smile. "My legs feel strong!" she shouted. "I can breathe again."

The preacher opened the chapel door and stepped out. He offered Chi his free arm, which she took. He turned to Luke.

"You coming?"

"I'm going to grab these leg braces." Luke congratulated himself for his quick thinking.

Reverend James escorted Chi through the door and allowed the door to close on Luke. Luke hesitated just a second to make sure they didn't turn back around, and then ran for the recorder. He had it turned off and in his backpack in less than eight seconds. He walked out the chapel door and right out the side door of the church without even saying goodbye.

CHAPTER 33

Reverend James walked into the church office hallway and opened the door of his office to find Maya Richards sitting in his chair. He came to a stop beside his desk and said the first thing that came to mind. "Hello, Maya."

Maya seemed upset. "Do you know what you're doing out there?"

Why is it that men think that women expect, or want, an answer to rhetorical questions? Reverend James was tired and stressed, true, but he still should have realized from the look on Maya's face that something was wrong. "I think I do." The preacher responded. Upon seeing the troubled look on Maya's face, the lightbulb went on, and he tried to recover. "I mean, yes—of course."

Silence.

Maya waited until Reverend James was quiet. "Why are you trying to come up with a plan to choose an order to heal people by yourself? You could have asked me to help."

Normally, Reverend James would respond. He was alert now, and wisely just nodded. He was starting to realize there was more to this conversation than she was saying.

"Picking numbers out of a basket? Really? What were you thinking?"

Reverend James recognized the rhetoric and was silent.

"That was the best you could come up with?"

"*I* picked the first five."

Maya rose out of the chair and walked over to him. "And you think that makes it better?" Maya softened her tone and paused. "I don't understand why you didn't ask for my help."

Maya took hold of his hands, guided him in front of his chair and gently shoved him into it. The preacher landed in the chair and watched as Maya dragged a chair from the other side of his desk. She placed it close to him and sat down.

"How do you think those people felt when you did that?"

Reverend James could still see the hurt and anger on their faces. What was he supposed to do? Still, now that Maya pointed it out—he understood what she meant.

"You think I hurt their feel..." The look on Maya's face stopped him in mid-sentence. "Yes, you're right. I hurt their feelings."

Reverend James expected Maya to be happy with his statement, but instead, he saw tears well up in her eyes. That's when it hit him.

"I hurt *your* feelings."

The tears rolled down Maya's cheeks.

"You came into the office and said you needed my help, and I got all excited." Maya looked him in the eyes and her bottom lip trembled. "Then you asked me for a pen and some paper." She tried to be strong, but she couldn't slow the tears.

Reverend James ripped a couple of tissues out of the box and handed them to her. He rolled his chair in close and put his arms around her, and she leaned into him. *I'm an idiot,* he thought.

"You're an idiot," she confirmed. He held her and waited. When she'd stopped crying, she pulled away from him and looked him in the eyes.

"I don't want to be just a secretary to you anymore, James."

Reverend James couldn't believe that he had made her feel this way. He searched for the right words, "Maya, you're not just—I mean, I didn't want to make you feel like…"

Then, like George Foreman, she hit the stumbling preacher with a proverbial brick.

"I love you, James!"

The preacher stared into Maya's eyes and was speechless. It didn't matter; Maya wasn't finished.

"I've been in love with you from the moment Thelma died. Before that, even."

Reverend James pulled away and continued to stare at Maya.

She hadn't planned on taking it this far, but now that she had, Maya decided it was time to let him know everything—and she wasn't going to hold any of it back. She had kept it inside for too long and today was the day.

"The truth is I've been in love with you even longer than that, but you were already in love with Thelma by the time I met you."

"Maya, you don't have to tell me all this—"

"Yes, I do," Maya interrupted. "Please just let me get this out, James. I've got to get this out. I've carried this guilt around for too long, and I can't do it, anymore. I should have taken this chance eight years ago, and I didn't because...because...because I felt so ashamed and guilty."

Maya seemed to crumble in front of the preacher's eyes, and the tears came harder.

Reverend James was confused. "Guilty? For what?"

The words tumbled out of Maya like a stone rolling down a mountainside. "Because part of me was glad that Thelma was gone." Maya's entire body shook, and she sobbed uncontrollably. "I'm sorry, James," she choked out through her waves of tears. "I'm so sorry. Please, don't hate me."

Reverend James' mind reeled with the statement. He felt his anger rising to consume him. He had been blind-sided by Maya's admission. Just when he was about to stand up and charge out of the room, he heard Thelma's voice in his head, clear as a bell. *Maya really likes you, you know.* The preacher shook his head and grabbed onto his desk as the memory continued, *if anything ever happens to me, you should ask her out.*

Reverend James remembered it now, the whole conversation. Thelma had said he and Maya would make a wonderful couple—if she were gone, of course. He had ended the conversation quickly. Not that there was anything wrong with Maya, he just couldn't imagine life without Thelma—but Thelma could. *Did Thelma know?* The preacher's mind was blown again as he wondered if Thelma could have had a premonition.

He didn't put much stock in that kind of stuff—but then he had never believed in healing before, either.

Reverend James looked at the weeping woman in front of him and suddenly, it all made sense. He had hired her to work in the office after Thelma had died. She never could keep a boyfriend, and he was always happy when she got rid of them. Over the last eight years, hadn't he taken every opportunity to include Maya whenever he could and *wasn't she always there when he asked?* She had asked him to go out when they were in the chapel, right after John died, and *he had been glad she did.*

He couldn't stand to see her cry anymore. "Maya…"

"Please forgive me, James. I loved Thelma, too, and I…"

"Maya, listen to me, please…"

"You can fire me if you need to, and I'll move or I can…"

Maya was so lost in the guilt of things she couldn't change that he suddenly realized the time for talking was over. He grabbed the startled woman by the shoulders and lifted her to her feet. Before she had a chance to say anything else, he wrapped his big, strong arms around her and kissed her.

"You really need to learn when to shut up." Before she could respond, he kissed her again. When they separated, he whispered in the gentlest tone she had ever heard, "I love you, too."

CHAPTER 34

Reverend James leaned forward in the chair across from his mother in her living room. Mary Matthews watched her son while she rocked back and forth in her chair. The conversation during dinner had been sparse. Reverend James had even turned down the carrot cake with cream cheese icing, his favorite dessert. Mary decided she had waited long enough.

"You want to talk about it?"

"About what, Momma?"

"Whatever it is that is making you sit there grinding your jaws like that."

Reverend James opened his mouth and rubbed both sides of his jaw, just below his ears. The tension there was painful. He hadn't noticed it until she'd mentioned it.

Mary waited as only a mother knows how to wait.

Reverend James dropped his hands to his knees and looked his mother in the eye. "I think I love Maya, Momma."

He expected a surprised look on his mother's face, but all he got was a knowing smile.

"Tell me something I don't know, child."

Reverend James was incredulous. "You know?"

"I'm your mother, James."

"But...if you knew, how come you didn't say anything?"

Mary leaned forward and answered with a question of her own. "What did you want me to say?

That I thought you should ask Maya out? That I've known Maya was in love with you for years?"

The preacher just blinked his eyes and tried not to fall out of his chair.

"Fifty-year-old men don't like their mommas buttin' into their love life, James." She laughed out loud. "Actually, that starts closer to ten years old."

"You're not upset?"

"Why would I be upset?"

He fumbled for the right words, "Well...you were very close to Thelma..."

"Thelma would be happy for the two of you, James." Mary sat back in her chair and rocked as the memories flowed in. "All Thelma ever wanted was for you to be happy. Your happiness was a large part of her joy."

"I miss her, Momma." His eyes glistened when the confession rolled out of his mouth. "I feel guilty for loving Maya."

"Well, then, that makes you ridiculous." Mary needed to get her child focused, and that statement did the trick.

"The last thing Thelma would want is for you to be sitting in that empty house being miserable. You *know* that." Mary let that comment sink in, and continued. "You've got to live for today, James. You know that, too." She watched her son nod his head. "I know you are not ridiculous, James, but you've been wallowing about your loss of Thelma long enough, and it has to end."

Reverend James wiped the tears from his eyes. "I'm sorry, Momma."

"Don't *I'm sorry, Momma* me, James. Out with the rest of it. I can see it in your eyes."

The preacher was going to deny that there was more. But the look on his mother's face and the question that had nagged him since the first time he'd healed that boy on the skateboard poured out of him.

"I don't deserve this...gift, Momma."

He looked so pitiful Mary almost backed off, but her instincts told her that her son was in desperate need of some tough love.

"You don't deserve it, or you don't want it?"

"I don't know. I just..." Reverend James realized there was a simple way to say it. "Why me?"

"I understand Father Kirk already told you who to ask, James."

Reverend James carved a wry smile into his face at the thought of the conversation that his mother must have had with his friend Patrick. The smile faded quickly, and his eyes sparkled with tears again.

"What is it, child?"

"Do you think I'm prejudiced?"

"Dear Lord in Heaven! Why on Earth would you ask a question like that?"

"Today, when I was choosing who to heal...I picked an Asian woman over a young black boy from my congregation. I felt like if I chose the boy...somehow I'd be showing favoritism to my own kind." Reverend James desperately tried to find a way to verbalize his dilemma. "At the same time, choosing her, I felt like I was betraying my own kind. I've never felt that way before." The preacher searched his mother's eyes. "Does that make any sense? What should I do, Momma?"

Mary blurted out her first thought. "I think you should pray, James. If you really have this gift, then God sent you this gift for a reason. It's up to you to figure it out."

Mary knew it wasn't her best answer, but she needed a minute to recover from these questions that had surprised her.

"I just can't seem to find the answer."

With that, Mary relaxed and smiled. "A great man once said; *'If you can't find the answer, you're not asking the right questions.'*"

"Dad."

"Well, he always laid claim to that, but I'm not sure who said it first." Mary's smile grew larger at the thought of her late husband, and then faded. "I remember a time when all you saw was people in need, James, not their color. That man has been gone since we lost Thelma." It was hard for Mary to watch her son react to that statement. Mary's heart fluttered, and she grabbed her chest, the emotion affecting her physically. She did her best to cover it up. "Losing John just broke you, James." She felt dizzy and took a deep breath.

"Momma?" James asked.

Mary nodded. "I just need a minute, James...this is hard for both of us." She took a deep breath and let it out. Then dizzy feeling passed, and she drilled into her son. "Find yourself again, James...in here." Mary indicated her heart. "Otherwise, you can never really help anyone...no matter how many people you heal."

CHAPTER 35

Luke Jones entered the living room of his house and gently set the backpack on the couch. He would have fixed himself a stiff drink to celebrate, but his money was gone. Luke wasn't worried about that now. The only thing on his mind was checking out the gold-mine recording of the Asian woman, Chi Long, walking without her leg braces. That was the proof that the healing worked, and he would have his ticket to a financial windfall.

Luke was so juiced for viewing the tape that he lost his grip on the video camera. It sprang up in the air as he tried to grasp it. Like a nightmare, Luke watched in slow motion as the camera began its descent to the floor. With an instant burst of adrenaline, Luke launched himself over the coffee table and crashed into the floor head first, his hands extended in front of him. Little white lights danced in front of his eyes, and his head exploded with pain. Luke was temporarily blinded but felt something in his hands. His vision returned a moment later, and he was elated. Just inches off the floor, curled in his hands, was the video camera.

The joy didn't last too long as the pain from hitting his head returned with a vengeance. Luke curled up in a ball and pulled the camera in to his body to protect it. *I almost needed the preacher to heal me a third time.* Luke winced at the thought when he remembered that Reverend James had already healed someone today.

Thomas John

The pain slightly eased as Luke rose to his knees, careful to safely place the video camera on the old Zenith console in front of the ancient Sony television. The fact that Luke didn't have a flat screen didn't bother him at all. He was certain he would have as many flat screens as he wanted soon. First, though, he checked his reflection in the dark screen of the Sony and couldn't see any blood. He was going to have a bump for sure. He rubbed the spot where he had stopped his fall with his forehead. Yup, there was going to be a bump, alright. The lump had already begun to rise.

Luke focused on the good stuff. He staggered to the closet to retrieve the audio-visual cables to enable the playback from the video camera to the Sony. On his way back to the television, it suddenly occurred to him that he was lucky he hadn't been drinking when he'd fumbled the camera. There was no way he could have saved the camera if he had been loaded. *The Lord works in mysterious ways,* he thought.

Luke turned on the Sony to allow it to warm up. He manually switched to channel three and the screen went blue. Luke attached the yellow video cable to the front of the television, followed by the red and white audio connectors. He attached the respective connectors to the video camera and turned it on. Nothing happened.

He was about to have a brain hemorrhage when he noticed the battery indicator showing no charge. He laughed at the near-catastrophe and opened up the power cord compartment and plugged in the machine.

It occurred to him that if the battery was dead, he might not have gotten a recording of the healing—that could have spelled disaster. But then he remembered the blinking red light, and felt confident that all was well.

Luke turned on the machine and rewound the tape to the beginning. When he heard it stop, he pressed the play button and raced to the couch. The pain echoed in his head with each beat of his heart. The screen flickered, and the playback began.

Luke watched himself walking away from the shelf and looking out the chapel window into the church. A few minutes rolled by that showed Luke fidgeting at the window and looking back at the camera constantly. To Luke, sitting on the couch, it felt like an eternity. The pain in his head didn't help. Then he watched the tape show him tensing up and the chapel door opening. On the television screen, Luke jumped into the path of Reverend James' vision to block him from seeing the blinking red light he had just discovered.

Luke watched as the recorded version of himself stepped out of the line of sight. He was pleased to see the camera angle was perfect. Chi Long removed the braces from her legs and Luke took them and set them in the pew. Reverend James had his back to the video camera, but the playback showed him extend his arms and place his hands on the woman's legs. A light flashed across Chi Long's body and was absorbed. The television screen filled with white light as it shot out of her. That was when Luke realized something was terribly wrong.

On the television screen was video Luke did not shoot. The playback showed Luke entering the chapel and removing the video camera from the backpack and placing it on the shelf. For lack of a better idea, Luke yelled at the television, "I didn't record that!"

The next scene on the television was Luke stumbling out of Al's Place and dropping his keys onto the parking lot. That was quickly followed by a wide angle shot of Luke's Chevy Caprice entering the intersection and slamming into the skateboarder, Tommy Hinkle. Luke could hear the thud of Tommy's body hit the car and the crunch of the young man's body landing on the pavement, his body broken and bleeding. Luke panicked and screamed at the television again, "Nobody taped that! Where is the healing?"

The picture on the television changed again; this time it showed Luke in the second-to-the-last row of the preacher's church, coughing loudly. There was a close-up of Luke taking the collection basket full of money in one hand and dropping his handkerchief into it with the other. He saw his fist curl around the money and stuff the hanky and the money into his pants. The video even showed him coughing directly into the face of the man standing behind him and dropping a one dollar bill into the basket.

Luke looked at the video camera and saw its green play light on. He froze in his seat when he looked back to the television screen, and the scene changed again. His mind raced with the knowledge that what he was seeing was impossible. He desperately wanted the scenes he was watching to stop, but he couldn't move.

The Healing of Reverend James

The television showed Luke driving an older Lincoln Continental through a stop sign and slamming into the side of Thelma Matthews' car. The screaming metal and exploding glass filled the screen, and Luke saw the two people inside the car being smashed together and violently bouncing off the interior. That was followed immediately by a close-up of Thelma's crushed skull and lifeless eyes.

Luke jumped up from the couch and screeched at the television. "Nobody could have taped that, this isn't possible—stop it!" The television screen changed again, and Luke was horrified by the picture.

Filling the screen was his girlfriend, Jennifer Santiago, in heavy labor and pushing hard to birth their child. Luke didn't know if it was the birth of Jasmine or Morgan, since he was not present for either. All he knew was Jennifer was screaming at the top of her lungs, "Luke, damn you, you promised you would be here!" Another labor contraction increased the volume and pitch of her screams.

She thrashed and screamed again; "Damn you to hell, Luke Jones; Damn you to hell, Luke Jones; Damn you to hell, Luke Jones!"

Luke couldn't take any more, and his brain exploded with fear and anger. He jumped to the television and ripped the camcorder away from it. He smashed the machine into the floor; the pieces flew in all directions. Luke spotted the mini-videotape and stomped on it. He crushed it with his feet and screamed through the sobs that wracked his body. "No, No, No!"

Again and again Luke stomped on the videotape until it was nothing more than a pile of plastic parts and celluloid tape strewn under his feet. Exhausted and confused, he fell to the floor, unable to stand even one moment longer, landing on his hands and knees.

Luke tried in vain to stop the tears that rolled down his face. He choked and gasped and tried to take a deep breath. His body shook and trembled, the shock of having seen the dark side of his life thrown in his face still reeling in his mind. That was when it happened.

The air seemed to get sucked out of the room, like a house just before a tornado hits, and everything went quiet. Luke looked up, and the ceiling and four walls seemed to get closer. The sound came from all four corners of the room, the ceiling, and the floor; Luke would never forget the deep, rumbling voice that reverberated to his very soul: "DAMN YOU TO HELL, LUKE JONES; DAMN YOU TO HELL."

CHAPTER 36

Jasmine and Morgan Jones were playing on the porch of their house when they saw their father pull into the driveway and park off to one side. Jasmine got up and opened the front door and yelled inside.

"Mom, Daddy's here."

Jennifer walked out the door and heard the familiar groan of the driver's side door of Luke's car. She came to a dead stop as there was almost nothing familiar about the man who stepped out of the Chevy Caprice.

Luke Jones was clean-shaven and neatly dressed. He closed the moaning door and smiled up at the three girls. "I'm going to get that fixed," he said.

He opened the rear door of the car and retrieved three narrow boxes from the back seat and tucked them under his arm. He closed the door and walked to the bottom of the stairs; the smile grew bigger as he went. Luke's eyes were sparkling, and there was a bounce to his step.

"You going to just stand there and stare?" Luke asked. "I have presents."

Jennifer put her arms around their girls and walked down the stairs. All three just stared at Luke.

"Hello, girls." Luke began. He placed two of the boxes on the ground and knelt in front of Morgan with the third. "These are for you, Morgan. I picked them for you because they remind me how bright and lovely you are."

Morgan was in shock for two reasons: first, because it had been so long since she'd heard her daddy talk so nice, and second, because she could not remember ever getting a gift from her father before.

She opened the box and squealed with delight. "Flowers!" She grabbed the three daffodils out of the box and shoved them up against her nose and inhaled deeply.

Luke wasted no time and grabbed the second box and handed it to Jasmine.

Jasmine took the box but could not take her eyes off her father.

"You were the hardest for me to figure what kind to get, Jasmine. I needed something lovely and strong, like you. I chose these, and I hope you like them."

Jasmine opened the box and gasped. Inside were three miniature sunflowers, full and beautiful. She could do nothing but stare into the box, look at her father, and stare at the flowers again.

Jennifer was dumbfounded. She asked the question, but already knew the answer, as hard as that was to believe. "Are you drunk?"

Luke laughed, and there was a twinkle in his eye. "No, I'm not drunk." He reached down and handed Jennifer the last box. His voice was soft and determined. "I will never be drunk again."

Jennifer took the box and tried to rationalize the impossible scene that unfolded before her eyes. She lifted the lid, and her breath left her. Inside were a half-dozen yellow roses—her favorite. The roses were beautifully surrounded by fresh cut greens and baby's breath.

"I wanted to get you two dozen, Jennifer," Luke said, "but I needed the rest of the money to fill the gas tank and my cousin couldn't afford to lend me any more." Luke reached into his pocket and handed her the keys to his car. "I want you to have the car, Jennifer. You and the girls need it more than I do."

Jennifer took the keys and knew she was dreaming. She looked into Luke's eyes. "You are drunk, aren't you?" She knew he wasn't. The three girls held their flowers and stared at the stranger in front of them.

"I went back to the diesel plant this morning and asked Bill Jenkins for my old job back. You remember Bill, from high school?"

Jennifer nodded.

"He said he couldn't hire an ex-con to do a job like that. So I got on my knees and begged. I told him I would take anything—anything at all."

Jennifer snapped out of her trance. "Girls, take your flowers inside."

"No, please." Luke challenged, then immediately softened his voice. "I mean, you're their mother, and if you think they should go inside, I agree."

Jennifer's mouth fell open.

"But I'm their father, and they need to know about my life—even the mistakes I've made—and I need to know what is happening in theirs." Luke looked down at his girls and struggled to keep his eyes dry. "Lord knows, I've missed too much already."

The girls looked at their mother. She hesitated, but nodded her approval.

Luke continued. "Bill said he had an opening in janitorial. I took it."

Jennifer couldn't believe her ears. "You got a job?"

"Third shift. Forty hours a week. I'm on probation for six months. If I screw anything up, I'm done." He saw the look on Jennifer's face and rushed to reassure her. "I won't screw anything up. I know it's hard for you to believe that, and that's my fault. I only ask that you see for yourself, over time."

"This is a lot for me to handle, Luke." Jennifer wanted to believe him, she truly did. She had been disappointed, majorly disappointed so many times before. Still, there was something different about him today. "I'm going to need a little time to...to…"

Luke interrupted her. "To trust me, I know, but I'm not done." Jennifer marveled at the gentle but direct tone he used. "I have to meet the preacher at the church tonight, but first I'm going to the courthouse to tell them about my new job so you can start to get child support checks right away. I know I'm way behind, and I'll have them take out extra each week so I can catch up."

Now Jennifer knew she was dreaming. Any extra money she got would be a godsend. She felt a little dizzy—and Luke was still talking.

"I filled out all the paperwork for my new job this morning. I don't get health benefits for three months, and when I do, I'll put the girls on my policy right away."

The girls could sense their mother's excitement and giggled. Jennifer was overwhelmed.

"Luke...Luke, please...take a breath. This is too much...I mean, it sounds too good to be true, but...what happened to you?"

Luke eyes glistened when he gazed into each of his girl's eyes and back to Jennifer. "I want us to be a family again."

She wanted to believe him. She needed to believe him. The past spoke to her, and she heard the cautionary voice in her head, but hoped.

"Jasmine, Morgan. Please give your father a hug and take the flowers inside before they dry up."

The girls jumped into Luke's outstretched arms so fast they nearly crushed the flowers. After a big hug, Jasmine took her mother's flowers and the two girls raced up the stairs and into the house, laughing the whole way in.

Jennifer watched the girls leave and turned back around to feel Luke give her a gentle kiss on the cheek. He backed away from his startled girlfriend.

"Forgive me, Jennifer. I've wanted to do that since I got here." He took her hand and held it in his. "You said if I could be the kind of man you fell in love with...that you would want to have a ring on your finger."

Jennifer could feel her heartbeat. Time seemed to stop, and she hung on every word Luke said.

"I don't expect you to believe all this right now. I know I haven't earned that. But one year from today, if I prove it all true, I will be asking you to wear that ring...and be my wife."

Jennifer just stood and gawked at him, this man who had given her two children and then abandoned her. She looked at him, but still couldn't believe that her wildest dreams might come true. She just couldn't believe it. She couldn't move. She couldn't speak.

Luke saw his girlfriend lost in her thoughts and realized he had probably said too much. He knew it was going to take time, and he had things to do before going to the church tonight.

"Anyway, you think about it, Jennifer. I need to get to the courthouse." Luke backed away, not wanting to take his eyes off what he now knew was the best thing that had ever happened to his life.

Jennifer tried to make sense of it all. She believed him, and she didn't know why. It just wasn't possible, not for Luke. *How could a person do a hundred-and-eighty-degree turn like that overnight?* She thought. *The only person I have ever seen do that was...Reborn!*

Jennifer's eyes popped open, and she screamed his name. "Luke!"

Luke stopped, and Jennifer looked into his eyes and suddenly it all became clear. His face was glowing. Jennifer felt like she was floating on air. She blurted out the thought that was prancing in her brain.

"Have you found God?"

Luke smiled. "Actually, Jennifer...I don't think God was lost." Luke shivered at the memory of the video playback last night. He winked at his girlfriend and said what he knew to be true. "He found me."

CHAPTER 37

Luke walked across the church parking lot satisfied with his day. He had accomplished a lot. *That's what happens when you're afraid to go to sleep at night, and you're sober.* He remembered throwing out the empty booze bottles and cleaning his house, after he recovered from his traumatic event.

He had cowered next to his television set and the crushed videotape for over an hour last night. The panic attack that followed *the event*, as he would forever refer to it, had made it hard to breathe or even move. Then, in the middle of all of that chaos, he had heard a thought pass through his brain. *You can change, Luke.*

The moment that thought crossed his mind, he stopped shaking and was able to stand. He started cleaning up his living room, and that little voice he had heard turned into a roar. *YOU CAN CHANGE.*

When he started to clean the kitchen, he thought about Jennifer and the girls, and the vision grew stronger yet. By the time he had cleaned the whole house and showered and shaved, it was nearly five a.m. He found clean clothes that he had forgotten he owned. He got dressed and went out in search of his cousin. From there, everything had gone so smoothly that it just didn't seem real. Shelly had loaned him eighty bucks so he could fill the tank with gas. He was at the diesel plant by seven a.m.

After getting a job—he still couldn't believe he'd gotten a job—he stopped and got the flowers for the girls and drove to Jennifer's. Once again, the events at Jennifer's house had gone so well it was like a dream. He felt like Ebenezer Scrooge, who had just found out Christmas wasn't over yet.

He had walked half a block away from Jennifer's house when he remembered the courthouse was in Mayville, New York, over seventeen miles away. He expected Jennifer to be upset when he went back and asked to borrow *her* car, but she just tossed him the keys, saying she'd known that he would be back.

He had spent most of the day tied up at the courthouse. But he had completed the necessary paperwork, dropped off the car at Jennifer's house, and was even a few minutes early for his appointment with Reverend James for the next healing.

He was walking across the church parking lot when the sound of a car that had rapidly slowed down and stopped, brought him out of the mental re-hash of his day. He turned and saw Jesus' black BMW 740Li pull over to the side of the road; the windows that faced him were rolled down.

Luke recognized the stunned faces of Jesus, Raymond, and Tony. He knew he shouldn't have done it, but he was in a great mood, so he had some fun.

"Hey, guys, good to see you again." He yelled across the parking lot. "Look, I've got a great idea. Let's get together real soon for a good game of baseball." Luke laughed hysterically and then screamed even louder. "You bring the bat!" He turned backward and tripped over the sidewalk leading to the side entrance of the church. He regained his balance, waved goodbye to the car, and went in

.

***

The three men in the BMW stared after him. Raymond turned to say something to Jesus, but stopped when Jesus yelled at him. "Not a word, Raymond. Not even one."

Jesus turned to Tony. "Not a word out of you, either." The two men just sat and stared at the church door.

Jesus' head reeled from what he had just seen. He didn't know what kind of voodoo crap was going on here, but he knew he couldn't let Luke get away with it. You let one guy slide on their repayment program, and the next thing you knew, everybody thought the money was free. Jesus couldn't figure out what had happened, and he didn't care.

He was pissed. More than pissed, really— seething. Now this thing got bumped up to a whole new level. The two women he had waiting at the house would just have to wait.

"Tony, take me to your house. I'm going to drop you and Raymond off."

Jesus took one last look at the church door Luke had walked through and rolled up the window. "I'm going to need the car tonight."

CHAPTER 38

Luke Jones had laughed when he'd entered the side door of the church, still congratulating himself for his amazing wit. Then he saw the young man they were supposed to heal tonight, and the laughter stopped.

Trevor, the young man that was second on the list to be healed, sat in the last pew of the church crying. When he looked up and saw Luke, he cried even harder.

"Luke." The preacher stood beside the open door of the chapel and waved at Luke to hurry. Luke hustled over.

***

Inside the chapel was a little girl in a wheelchair. A woman knelt beside her. Reverend James made the introductions. "Luke, this is Tasha Roberts and her mother, Claire. Tasha was sent home from the hospital today and is under Hospice care. They are telling her that her time is very limited."

"I heard about the miracles you performed here from my cousin, Anita Tomasina," Claire said. "For obvious reasons, I believed her. I mean, she can *see*. It doesn't seem possible—well, I guess I mean that I was hoping that you could help Tasha."

"I understand, Mrs. Roberts."

Luke smiled but couldn't shake the look on Trevor's face. Betrayal. He was second on the list, but not anymore. Apparently, the needs of this little girl trumped Trevor's needs. That meant everybody else on the list would be bumped back as well. He knew and did understand Tasha's need, but there was another thought that grew in his brain. *How often is this going to happen? What if two people in desperate need showed up at the same time?*

The preacher knew it was terrible to have told Trevor he would have to wait a day. Worse still, the thought that this could happen again—the possible snowball effect was mind-boggling. That day in the hospital—the day he'd realized that he could heal only one person a day—he knew that something like this was not only possible, but probable. He had hoped that he would have more time before it happened.

The preacher relived that day in the chapel, the day the vision of his great-grandfather told him there would be *conditions* on this gift. *A gift?* He was beginning to think this was not a gift at all. If he had known what the conditions were before he had been given this gift, would he have taken it? He changed his mind about that every other second.

There was a good side, too. Miraculous things had been done; people had been healed. The good outweighed the bad, right? Reverend James decided once again that he must live in the present and accept the task in front of him. No matter how difficult the current situation was, he needed to be grateful it wasn't any worse. He knew from experience that it could always get worse.

"Yes, Mrs. Roberts, I think we can…"

"Please, call me Claire."

"Claire. I believe Luke and I can help your daughter."

Claire sobbed. "Oh, thank God!"

"In order for us to do that, I'm going to need you to wait in the other room."

Claire looked stunned. Her daughter heard the comment and panicked. "Mommy, don't leave me!"

"I'm not going to leave you, honey." Claire knelt and wrapped her arms around her terrified daughter. She gave the preacher a look that told him she was going nowhere.

"You don't understand, Claire...the healing won't work with you in the room."

"He's right," Luke added, "we've tried it with other people in the room and it just won't work. It has to be just the two of us."

"Why is that?"

Reverend James and Luke looked at each other. No one had questioned that condition before, and it surprised them both. They didn't get a chance to respond, because the chapel door swung open.

Maya Richards was wild-eyed and breathing hard. "Reverend James, thank God you haven't left."

"Maya, we're in the middle of..."

"It's your mother...she's had a heart attack!"

"What? When...where is she?"

"WCA Hospital. James...it's bad."

The preacher headed for the door. "Luke, let's go!"

"What about my daughter?" Claire asked.

"Maya, please stay with Claire and Tasha. I'll be back as soon as I can." He was gone. Luke hesitated for just a second, and then followed him.

CHAPTER 39

Reverend James charged into his mother's room with Luke in tow. They stopped when the doctor turned to them. "May I help you?"

Reverend James saw his mother lying in bed, still in the emergency room, her eyes closed.

"This is my mother. Hi, Momma, it's James."

"I know who it is. It's my heart wearing out, not my head."

"Hello," the doctor said, "we're waiting for a room to become available.

"Doctor, please," Mary opened her eyes, "wait outside. I'll just be a minute."

"I'm afraid I can't do that."

"How come you're afraid?" Mary responded. "I'm the one dying here. Now, please, let me say goodbye to my child."

The doctor chose not to argue and left. The preacher grabbed Luke's hand and pulled him over to his mother's bedside. He put his hands together and prayed.

"Don't you touch me, James!"

"Momma, what do you mean? I can help you."

Mary turned to Luke and stared at him for a moment. *He looks brighter,* she thought. "Luke, you look...different." She struggled to get the words out.

"Yes, Ma'am," Luke answered.

"I'm glad." Mary gave him a smile. She was sure she knew the reason. She had seen the faces of many people who had discovered a new meaning, a love unlike any they had ever known before. She truly was happy for Luke.

"I need to talk to my son…please?"

Luke nodded and left.

"Momma, please." Reverend James pleaded.

"I'm sorry, James, no. I've been looking forward to meeting Jesus my whole life, and you're not going to take that from me now."

"I love you, Momma. I need you here."

"I love you, too, James. It's my time. I'm tired, James…old and tired." Mary's voice was weak, and she thanked God she had this time with her son. "I miss your father…I've missed him for far too long. I have signed a DNR form, James." Mary reached out and took his hand. "I'm not afraid."

Reverend James knew what a *Do Not Resuscitate* form was—and what it meant. "*I'm* afraid, Momma." The tears streamed down his face and Mary pulled her son into her arms one last time. They clung to each other and held on tight.

"I've got something for you, James," Mary whispered in his ear. The preacher pulled away. "Around my neck…take it." she said. "Remember this, James…it can only be given, it can never be taken."

The preacher reached behind her neck and gingerly removed a gold chain. Hanging on the bottom was the most beautiful golden cross. He knew the cross had belonged to his father, Quentin Matthews. It had been a gift from *his* father, James' grandfather, on the day Quentin Matthews had become a preacher. He had rarely seen it since his father died. Mary never took it off and always wore it under her clothes, next to her heart.

"Let me see you put it on, James."

He did as his mother requested. It was thick and heavy, much larger than he remembered. It hung right over his heart. "It's beautiful, Momma. I will wear it—always."

Mary struggled to continue. "Let it remind you of the three gifts God gave us all, James: Faith, Love, and Hope. If you have nothing else in life but these three...you can have the most wonderful life."

"I'll remember, Momma, I will."

Mary's eyes opened wide in wonder, and she stared past her son.

"He's here, James, he's here!"

The preacher turned to look and saw nothing. Alarms started beeping, and the preacher looked at the monitors.

"Momma! Momma!"

Mary Matthews could hardly be heard. "I'm going home James...I'm going home." Mary smiled and took a deep breath. It was her last. She exhaled, and the monitors went flat.

Reverend James watched his mother's eyes fade. He began to pray.

A moment later, the doors burst open, and the doctor and two nurses ran in. They stopped when they saw the preacher, still holding his mother's hand, bent in obvious prayer. The doctor calmly walked over and silenced the alarms.

CHAPTER 40

Reverend James strode out of the hospital room and charged passed Luke.

Luke ran after him. "Where are you going?"

"To the chapel."

"But your mother?" Luke asked.

The preacher stopped at the elevator and pressed the down button.

"She's in God's hands now, Luke. There's a little girl that needs mine."

"I'm sorry, Reverend James, I truly am. For your loss, I mean. I know right now may not be a good time, but there's something I really need to talk to you about."

"You're right, Luke. Now is not a good time."

The elevator arrived, and Reverend James stepped in. Luke wasn't happy to be shut down like that, but joined the preacher in the elevator. He would have to bide his time.

***

Reverend James walked into the chapel and was stunned to discover that Maya was the only one in there. She turned from her seat in the pew and rose when Luke walked in.

"Where are Claire and Tasha?"

"They went home."

"They went home?" the preacher repeated. "Why did they do that?"

Maya didn't want to answer, but spit it out as fast as she could. "After you left, Claire got angry...furious, really. She yelled at me and asked what kind of man would try to separate her from her dying child. Then she said that you abandoned her child when you ran off to see your mother and she wasn't going to hang around and wait for somebody who would do a thing like that.I'm sorry, James."

"It's okay, Maya." Reverend James was distressed by Claire's reaction, but Maya was already upset enough.

"How's Mary?" Maya saw the instant reaction on the two men's faces, and her tears flowed. "Oh no! Not Mary!"

Reverend James wrapped Maya in his arms and held her tight. "She wouldn't let me heal her, Maya. She stopped me. Made Luke leave the room."

"That's exactly what happened," Luke offered. "She made me leave."

"Maya, she told me that she knew it was her time, and she was ready to go."

Maya pulled back and searched his eyes. "She said that she missed her husband terribly, and she didn't want my gift." He continued, "So, Luke and I hurried right back here after...after she was gone."

"You just left her there?"

"Yes, but I knew Tasha needed me as soon as possible. I didn't realize that she had left."

"James, there are arrangements to be made.You know that."

"I know that. Now that Tasha is gone," the preacher looked through the window, "there is a young man out there that could really use our help."

Maya had forgotten about Trevor. It made perfect sense to her. She wiped the tears from her eyes and knew what to do.

"Then I'll go to the hospital and take care of things until you can get there." Maya had helped with many funeral arrangements and knew all the procedures. She gave Reverend James a peck on the cheek and turned to go.

"Thank you, Maya," Reverend James replied.

Maya stopped at the door. "There was something I wanted to tell you...but, I can't seem to remember what it is." Maya was rewinding her tapes but couldn't remember. "It seemed like it was important. What was it?"

"Don't worry about it now, Maya. With everything that's been going on, I'm surprised I can remember my own name."

"Are you sure you're alright? I could stay for a little bit if you need me."

"I need you." The preacher declared. "More than ever, I need you. I would like it very much if you would make sure they take care of Momma until I can get there."

"I'll make sure everything is done right, James." She smiled and left.

Luke had been watching the scene and shot the preacher a knowing smile.

"What?"

"You like her," Luke said.

The preacher's first reaction was to tell Luke it was none of his business, but when he looked at him, there was something...different. "I like her."

"More than that."

"More than what?" Reverend James asked.

"Like." Luke's smile grew larger.

Reverend James thought he should be upset with Luke, but he wasn't. Luke seemed to have lost that bitter, cutting edge that had formerly pressed all his buttons.

"What is going on with you, Luke?"

"Oh, now—don't avoid the question, Reverend James. We're talking about you and Maya, now. C'mon, it's another four-letter-word, and it begins with L."

The preacher stared at Luke and saw no signs of malice. Still, his mother had just died, and he was in no mood to play these games—especially with Luke Jones.

"Enough, Luke. We have a young man to heal."

Luke got serious. "I need to talk to you first."

"I don't want to talk. I want to heal this young man, and then I need to get to the hospital and take care of the final arrangements for my dead mother."

"I need to talk to you right now."

"You are not hearing me, Luke. Not now. There are more important things going on here than whatever it is you think you need to say to me." Reverend James stepped toward the door and Luke grabbed his arm.

"Please!"

"Let go of me!" Reverend James swept Luke's hands off of his arms.

Luke fell to the floor on his knees.

"What is wrong with you, Luke?"

Seemingly out of nowhere, Luke burst into tears. "I'm sorry I killed your wife!" Luke choked out. "I need to tell you how sorry I am that I killed your wife."

Reverend James was in disbelief. Luke's entire body shook. The pain was apparent in his eyes. It took Luke just seconds to go from smiling to weeping—and here he was, apologizing for the unforgivable. The preacher was in shock, and everything moved in slow motion. He couldn't speak.

Luke, on the other hand, couldn't talk fast enough. The guilt and grief that had been numbed for the past eight years was impossible to stop.

"It was all my fault. She didn't deserve to die. She shouldn't be dead...she wouldn't be dead if I wasn't drunk, and I'm so sorry..." Luke's sobs cut off his air and he gasped and sputtered. "I wish I could trade places with her, Reverend. I wish I was dead and she was alive. I can't stop thinking about it. I can't stop dreaming about it. I'm so sorry..."

Reverend James watched the tortured man in front of him. He hated this man. He had never hated anyone in his whole life like he hated Luke. He suddenly felt the weight of that hate. The past eight years of despising this man flashed before his eyes. Hatred for Luke had quickly followed every loving memory he had ever had of Thelma. Now that he thought about it; he hadn't been able to enjoy the fond memories of his dead wife, because every time he thought about her, he thought about him.

The preacher's mind sped up, and he saw the effects of those hate-filled years. He had been less patient. It was harder to counsel his congregation. He was numb to the needs of others. He hadn't been able to ask Maya out—or even feel that kind of love. *There is no room for love in a heart filled with hate.* The thought rocked his world even further. How many times had he heard his father and grandfather say those very words, and not heard them, or at least not applied them to himself.

Reverend James remembered what his mother had said just an hour ago when she was dying; *faith, love, and hope: if you have nothing else but these, you can have a wonderful life.*

The preacher looked at the cross he had torn from the wall just weeks ago. He had judged God's will for him and been given this gift. But it wasn't really a gift, was it? Who was he to choose who should live and who should die? Who was he to stand in judgment of the Lord?

In a sickening rush, Reverend James understood the conditions of his gift. Luke Jones had to be his witness, and no one else was allowed to be present. It was about love—love for his fellow man...this man. For he could see now that unless he could rid himself of this hate for Luke, he could never enjoy true love again.

The preacher fell to his knees and wrapped his arms around Luke. With his tears came the words that would set his heart free, and he meant every one.

"I forgive you, Luke."

Luke cried out in relief and joy, and the two men held each other while the tears washed away the guilt and hate that had turned their lives sour. After a time, they released each other and sat back on their knees. Neither man spoke, yet both knew that they felt lighter and stronger than they had just moments before.

Luke spoke first. "You look awful, in a good kind of way."

"Thanks. You do, too."

They lingered there for a moment, and Reverend James nodded toward the chapel door.

"You ready to help that young man?"

Luke nodded. "Yes I am, Reverend James. Yes I am."

CHAPTER 41

Trevor lay in the middle of the floor with his head toward the altar. He had explained that his back hurt too badly to sit any longer. He had had a rare back infection called an epidural abscess: a pocket of infection, wrapped around his spine, that would have killed him if the surgeons hadn't cleaned it out in time. It had required five laminectomies, removal of the top third of five of his vertebrae, to allow the infection to be cleaned out. He could barely walk and could sit for only short periods of time. He had been sitting for way too long today and was in horrible pain.

The two men had cleaned themselves up as well as they could, but their eyes were puffed and red.

Trevor hadn't asked any questions, but he had one now. "Is this going to hurt?"

"No, it's not going to hurt," Luke answered.

They sat on the ends of the second row of pews, opposite each other. Then they dropped to their knees on each side of the young man.

"You ready?" Reverend James asked.

Trevor nodded and took a deep breath. The preacher put his hands together and whispered a quick prayer. He brought his hands down and gently laid them on Trevor's chest.

Nothing.

Reverend James and Luke looked at each other in shock. Luke pointed to himself and shook his head no, just in case the preacher thought he had done something. Reverend James shrugged his shoulders and put his hands together in prayer again. He placed them on Trevor's chest again.

Still nothing.

"Who's that?" Trevor pointed toward the door.

The two men turned toward the chapel door. They had not heard it open.

Jesus Julio Juarez had been standing in the open doorway. He stepped into the chapel. He wore gloves and had a nine millimeter semi-automatic pistol in his right hand and a taser in his left. He pulled the gun up and shot a round through the middle of Trevor's chest. Reverend James and Luke jumped to their feet as Jesus shot the preacher twice, once in the gut and once in the chest. He crumpled and went down hard.

Luke leaped at Jesus, who rewarded his bravery with seven hundred and fifty thousand volts of electricity. Luke went rigid and then collapsed into the pew. Jesus grabbed Luke and propped him against the wall in a sitting position.

Luke twitched and jerked, his mouth opening and closing. No sound escaped, but tears rolled down his cheeks.

Jesus stepped over to the two men he had just shot and kicked each in turn. There was no response. He wasn't concerned. He was a marksman and an expert with a pistol. He knew the bullets had hit their marks

"Oh, Luke, look what you've done." Jesus pointed at the men. "You killed these two men with your stolen gun." Jesus knelt next to Luke and got in his face. "All you had to do was pay your debts, amigo, but nooo. You have to be a wise guy. First you don't pay; then you go walking around town making jokes about baseball bats and insulting the people that loaned you the money in the first place."

Jesus sat back and laughed. "I should thank you, though—and I do. True, I don't get the nine hundred dollars you owe me, and that is a shame. But when this story hits the news, I won't even have to go collect on my loans for the next two years. The people who owe me will be tripping over each other to bring the money to me."

He set the gun on the pew and took off his suit coat. He pulled a small plastic package out of the inside pocket and unwrapped it to reveal a cheap, clear, plastic rain coat. He stood and put the raincoat on and snapped it closed all the way up to his neck and pulled on the hood. He sat back down next to Luke and carefully pulled the sleeves of the raincoat far down over his gloves.

He picked up the gun and placed it in Luke's hand. "I'm sorry my outfit is not very attractive, but these are very expensive clothes. No need to ruin my threads just because you were filled with remorse, and you killed yourself."

Jesus' pulse quickened when he looked into Luke's desperate eyes. He was already jacked up from killing the other two, but there was just something over-the-top about being eye to eye with someone who knew they were going to die.

He savored the power and ultimate control of the moment. Jesus brought Luke's hand up, so the gun was under his chin and aimed up at his head. He had one more parting gift for Luke.

"Don't worry about your girlfriend, Luke. I plan on taking good care of her." He was almost nose to nose with Luke. "That Jasmine is a little cutie, too. Who knows—in five or six years…" He saw the anger and terror erupt in Luke's eyes, followed by the moment he had been waiting for: total helplessness. Jesus leaned back and reveled in the moment just a second longer, then pulled the trigger.

Jesus was careful to let go of the gun right after he pulled the trigger and let it fall naturally. It had to look natural. He stepped away from the mess and carefully pulled the raincoat up over his head and down his arms away from his body. He folded the raincoat in on itself and let the gloves come off with it. He retrieved a plastic bag from his suit coat and put the whole mess in it. Reaching into his other pocket, he put on clean gloves.

He stopped at the door and surveyed the room once more. Content his plan was complete, he allowed himself a satisfied smile.

Now that, he thought, *is how you play God!*

CHAPTER 42

Maya Richards was exhausted. She had been at the hospital for four and a half hours and had taken care of all the arrangements for Mary Matthews. She was on her way out the door, wondering what was taking Reverend James so long, when one of the nurses, a member of her choir, spotted her.

The nurse came crying and screaming down the hall. It took a few minutes to calm the nurse down enough to understand anything she said. When she finally told Maya about the shooting at the church, Maya clung to her for dear life and wept.

When Maya could walk again, she headed for the morgue and steeled herself for the unthinkable. She would have to bury Reverend James with his mother. *How could Luke have done something like that?* She had seen them together just hours earlier and everything had looked fine—with Luke, anyway. It seemed so unreal—so wrong. Maya had to stop along the way and gather her strength.

She made it to the morgue and asked to see James' body. The attendant took a long time at the computer screen and kept apologizing for the delay. Maya was lost in thought and hadn't noticed the unusually long wait.

"There's no one here by that name."

The man's fingers continued to work the keyboard while Maya struggled to make sense of the statement.

"I see what the problem is, ma'am," the man continued. "He's not dead, yet. I mean, he's in surgery."

"He's in surgery?" Maya heard the words but couldn't make sense of those, either. A moment later, the words connected with her traumatized brain and she shouted. "He's in surgery!"

"Yes. First floor west."

"First floor west?"

"Yes, ma'am, take that elevator you just came down, up to the first floor, hang a left, and you'll find the waiting room for surgery about fifty yards down that hall."

Maya left, and arrived in the empty waiting room moments later. The shock tried to grab her, and she hit her knees.

Five minutes and a prayer of thanks later, she knew what to do. She pulled her phone out and called her prayer chain. With one quick phone call, she would wake up an entire congregation in less than twenty minutes. Obviously, Reverend James was in a fight for his life, and she would see to it that he got all the help she could muster. She called Father Patrick Kirk herself.

***

Forty-five minutes later, the waiting room was overflowing with concerned parishioners. Most prayed in groups; some talked quietly amongst themselves. Father Kirk sat with Maya, and they held hands. Maya had explained that the nurses told her that the situation was very serious, and they expected the surgery to last for some time. They were unable to give her an estimate.

Father Kirk was familiar with many in the congregation, and he and Maya spent the next six hours making the rounds. They would sit and pray with one group, and then talk with another. At one point, about four and a half hours in, the entire group held hands and prayed in unison. The people spilled out into the hallway, and everyone present felt the energy their combined spirit created.

It was early Thursday morning, and those who had to work later that day reluctantly headed home for a couple hours of sleep. Maya promised to send word as soon as they heard something. By six a.m., there were still a dozen people left. Reverend James had been in surgery for eight and a half hours.

Father Kirk and Maya had one corner of the waiting room to themselves. Neither was going anywhere until they heard some news.

"So, how is Susan Erikson doing?" Maya asked.

Father Kirk avoided Maya's eyes. "She has some…challenges to overcome."

"Two years in a wheelchair and suddenly you can walk again. I'd have some challenges, too," Maya responded.

The priest was uncomfortable, and Maya knew it.

"What's wrong, Father?"

Father Kirk hesitated. "I wouldn't normally discuss my parishioner's private matters, but it's going to be public knowledge soon anyway." He took a deep breath and continued, "Susan's husband filed for divorce."

"Divorce?"

"Yes."

Maya was shocked. "But it was only two or three weeks ago! She can walk again…that *had* to be good news for them both, wasn't it?"

"Well, yes…but not like I'd hoped. You see, now that Susan can walk again, her husband feels she can take care of herself. He claims to be in love with the woman he has been having an affair with and wants to marry her. He filed the paperwork yesterday."

Maya was silent. She had pictured the effect of Susan's healing much differently. She changed the subject. "What about the blind woman, Anne?"

"Anita Tomasina?"

"Anita."

"I wish I could say everything was wonderful there, but she is facing some challenges of her own." Father Kirk leaned in. "Besides the sensory overload…she's been blind her whole life and, well, you can imagine: color, shapes, people, and animals. I can't even conceive what it must be like. She's never seen her own face before."

"Is that a bad thing?" Maya asked.

"Not necessarily," he hedged, "but she's going to lose many of her benefits."

"What do you mean?"

"She's no longer blind. She received all kinds of benefits through government programs: Braille books, transportation assistance, and things like that. Think about it, Maya, she doesn't drive. She doesn't read. She wouldn't even be able to read the booklet to take her driver's test unless it was in Braille; then she couldn't read the street signs. Not to mention what it would be like to *see* traffic. The challenge Anita faces is staggering. Basically, she has to relearn everything."

Maya pondered the ramifications of what she'd just heard. The intention of healing someone seemed like it should be a gift, but this didn't sound like a gift at all. *Unintended consequences,* she thought. For every action, there is an equal and opposite reaction. There were dozens of ways to say it, but the truth was, life was unpredictable. She'd seen it over and over again in her forty-nine years.

Maya heard her name being called and looked up to see a police officer standing in the hall next to a large man in a suit.

"Are you Maya Richards?" the officer asked.

"Yes."

"I'm Shelly Jones and this is Detective Juliano. We're here about the shootings at Reverend James' church last night."

"Actually, *I'm* here about the shootings," the detective said. "Officer Jones came along since she knew who you were. Thank you, Officer. I can take it from here."

"Officer Jones?" Maya asked. "As in Luke Jones?"

Shelly nodded. "First cousins."

"First cousins?" Maya could see the bloodshot eyes and the pain they carried.

"There's no way Luke did those horrible things, Ma'am."

"Officer Jones! Time for you to go!" Detective Juliano barked.

"I'm sorry, Detective. A drunk, yes. A murderer…no way!"

The detective stepped in between Maya and Shelly and shouted his order. "Go!"

Officer Jones turned and walked away. When she rounded the corner of the hallway, the detective turned to Maya.

"I'm sorry, Ms. Richards. I was afraid of that."

"Please, call me Maya."

The detective continued. "Maya, I'm here because of the shootings at Reverend James' church last night."

"I understand, Detective. I'd like to help, but right now I'm waiting for Reverend James to get out of surgery."

"Not a problem, Maya." The detective reached into his pocket and pulled out a business card. "I just wanted to give you my card and ask you to call me, say…sometime this week for an interview. Obviously, we need to get some information pertaining to those involved."

Maya was relieved he wasn't going to try to interview her now. "I can do that."

"Thank you." The detective walked around Maya and made a bee-line for Father Kirk. Maya watched the detective hand Father Kirk his business card. Seconds later, she heard her name again.

Maya turned around and saw a man dressed in scrubs looking at her.

"Maya Richards?"

Maya nodded.

"I'm Dr. Dennison. Are you Reverend James Matthews' relative?"

"Reverend James doesn't have any relatives; they're all dead." Maya heard her words and was stunned by the truth of the statement. A tear rolled down her cheek. "I'm his...secretary."

The doctor hesitated. "Since he has no family...I suppose I could give you the information."

"I understand the privacy laws, Doctor. There *is* no one else to tell."

"Very well, then. I'm afraid Reverend Matthews' situation is very tenuous at the moment." Dr. Dennison searched for the right words.

"Just give me the facts, Doctor. I know it's not good."

"He was shot twice," Dr. Dennison began, "once in the chest, and once in the abdomen. The bullet in the chest, well...the bullet never made it to his heart." Dr. Dennison searched for the right words again. "Apparently, the bullet struck a cross that Reverend Matthews was wearing. Somehow, this prevented the bullet from...from doing any internal damage other than some severe bruising."

"I don't understand," Maya said.

"I'm afraid I don't either, Ms. Richards. I've been doing this for twenty-three years and frankly, I've never seen anything like it."

"What do you mean?"

"This cross that the preacher was wearing, it appears to be eighteen-karat gold. The bullet struck right in the middle of it and stuck there. How it didn't pass through the cross is beyond anything I can explain. Gold is a soft metal. It shouldn't have stopped the bullet."

"Can I see the cross?" Maya asked. She was amazed by what she'd heard. But after living the events of the past few weeks, she thought nothing seemed impossible anymore.

"The cross is evidence in a murder investigation, I'm afraid, but there's more I need to tell you."

Maya nodded. "Please, continue."

"The force of the impact bruised his heart, and also caused the cross to embed into the top layers of Reverend Matthews' skin. He's going to have a scar, in the shape of that cross, right over his heart."

"You said it bruised his heart?"

"Yes."

"Is that bad?"

"Well, it's certainly not good, and he will have to remain in ICU for some time, but there are other issues, as well, relating to the gunshot wound to the abdomen."

Maya was blank, her mind still reeling from what she had already heard. She managed a nod.

"There are a number of internal injuries, due to the trajectory of the bullet, most of which will heal with time. However, his spinal cord was severed."

He had Maya's full attention now.

"Reverend Matthews will be paralyzed from the waist down, permanently, I'm afraid."

The words echoed through Maya's brain. She closed her eyes and prayed for strength.

"One more thing you need to know," the doctor continued, "Reverend Matthews coded on the table, twice. We got him back both times, obviously, but the second time was of longer duration."

"Coded? You mean he died?"

"No, Ma'am, we were able to resuscitate him both times."

"How long was he...out for?"

"The only concern I have was the second time. We worked on him for eleven and a half minutes before we got him back."

"Eleven and a half minutes?" It was the best she had to offer.

"The next forty-eight to seventy-two hours are critical. We'll know a lot more about any complications by then, although nothing is certain at the moment." The doctor left.

Maya stood by herself in the hall. Considering all she had been told, it was amazing she was still on her feet. She wandered toward the waiting room, passing the departing detective, who had finished his conversation with Father Kirk.

She reached out for Father Kirk's hands, and he took them and held on.

"Father Kirk, will you please pray with me?"

"Yes, Maya, of course."

Maya and Father Kirk sat down and prayed for their friend.

EPILOGUE

Three days had passed since Reverend James had been shot. Maya had waited six hours after the conversation with Dr. Dennison to be allowed to come to his side, and had only left for bathroom breaks. The staff had told her that she could go down to the waiting room to lie down, but she had refused, preferring to sleep in the chair in order to be as close as possible to this man she loved.

Her lower back was sore, and her hip hurt from sleeping in the chair, but that didn't matter to her. She had been there for forty hours, and she would be there as long as it took. The first thing the preacher was going to see when he opened his eyes was her eyes; there was no other option. Maya knew this was only the beginning of a challenging journey, and she had spent every moment steeling herself to be ready.

The nurses had come and done what nurses do, checking vital signs, changing bandages, and changing IV bags. The doctors had come and read the charts and gone about their business.

Maya was asleep when she first felt the movement. His hand twitched in hers, and she awoke to find Reverend James looking into her eyes.

"Hello, James," she said.

His only response was a single tear that rolled down his cheek.

Maya had squeezed his hand and thanked God for this gift of life. For this, indeed, was the gift for which she had prayed. She had prayed to have this man in her life, in whatever way the good Lord willed it. Her prayers had been answered. The work could begin, a labor of love that would fill the rest of her days.

Maya Richards had been given the only thing she had asked for: to be a loving and faithful force in the healing of Reverend James.

THE END

ACKNOWLEDGEMENTS

I must first thank Ray Flynt, author of the BRAD FRAME MYSTERIES, for answering a text from a friend he had not heard from in years and agreeing to help with my first draft. He stayed with me even after reading my challenged first chapters, and gently guided me through much of the process.

To my wife Diane, who helped rewrite and edit, and listened to the non-stop struggling of a fledgling writer. The prologue was born from her suggestion, and the end of the book is heavily flavored by her input. As is true of my life, she made everything about this book, better.

I would like to thank those that read the completed work and gave of their valuable time to comment: Ray Flynt, Diane Kelly, Dale Lehnig, Thomas Kelly and Caitlin Kelly. Special thanks to Joe and Sue Kelly for their support and to Wydetta Carter for her input.

And of course, thanks to my mother, Susan Kaliszewski, who gave me a love of the English language and the written word.

Thomas John

CPSIA information can be obtained at www.ICGtesting.com
Printed in the USA
LVOW08s2122260715

447743LV00001B/4/P

9 780996 392402